Intelligence Analysis for Problem Solvers

Acknowledgments

We are grateful to the Office of Community Oriented Policing Services (COPS Office) for commissioning this manual, which is intended to be a companion volume to our earlier publication, *Crime Analysis for Problem Solvers: In 60 Small Steps*, which was also commissioned and published by the COPS Office. We thank our many colleagues and friends on whose work we have drawn. Special thanks are due to those who supplied material for inclusion: Christopher Bruce (Step 41), Mangai Natarajan (Step 20), Jerry Ratcliffe (Step 4), and Rashi Shuhkla (Step 43). Daryn Beauchesne, Leonard Miranda, Kristen Miggins, Andy Mills, Nanci Plouffe, Karin Schmerler, John Stedman, and Julie Wartell took part in a meeting, graciously hosted by the Chula Vista Police Department, to discuss our plans for the manual. Finally, we are grateful to Christopher Bruce and Andy Mills for their detailed commentary on the first draft of the manual.

John E. Eck

Ronald V. Clarke

Contents

Read This First

The 9/11 Commission famously criticized the country's intelligence agencies for failing to "connect the dots" before the attack—that is, for failing to detect a pattern in the scattered items of information about the hijackers that had come to the attention of various federal and state agencies. The resulting calls for intelligence reform were at first confined to the nation's security agencies, the FBI and the CIA. Soon police leaders began to argue that their agencies, too, had a vital role in addressing terrorism and that they must be included in the loop.

Terrorism may have raised the profile of police intelligence, but it is not the main reason for improving its use. Police intelligence has a far wider role in public safety, crime reduction, and order maintenance. This wider role is explored throughout this manual. Unfortunately, the word "intelligence" also raises public fears that secretly collected police information will be used to subvert individual liberties and democratic institutions. We will touch on these concerns later; here, we should explain why we wrote the manual, who it is for, and what it covers.

What is this manual about and who is it for?

As we discuss in Step 1, intelligence analysis is "a process for making sense of a diverse array of information about crime problems created by offender groups, with the goal of reducing crime." Numerous books and manuals for crime analysts are available that describe how to process data to guide police anti-crime tactics and strategies. In contrast, most writing on police intelligence focuses on data gathering and sharing, administration, and legal requirements. These are all important topics, but they do not help the analyst **analyze**, i.e., make sense of the data in order to glimpse behind the veil of a criminal enterprise.

Our manual fills this gap by providing a practical guide to intelligence analysis, much like our earlier manual on crime analysis written for the Center for Problem-Oriented Policing. In writing this manual, it soon became clear that police intelligence has a much larger mission than simply finding out who is up to no good, who they hang out with, what they are about to do, and where they can be found. These are the sorts of questions we normally expect police intelligence to address. However, there are other questions that intelligence analysis can effectively address, such as: How do offenders commit their crimes? What circumstances help them commit their crimes? And, what countermeasures might prevent them from doing so? In short, we look beyond the "who" to address "how," "when," "where," and "what."

This manual fuses aspects of intelligence analysis with Problem-Oriented Policing. The links between the two have been ignored in the past, with the exception of Jerry Ratcliffe's book referenced below. However, knowing how intelligence analysis can help solve problems and how problem solving can improve the effectiveness of intelligence analysis will aid any police practitioner interested in reducing crime or disorder.

This manual is not intended to serve the entire law enforcement community. Nor does it describe all facets of intelligence. Rather it focuses on the **analysis** of intelligence, and we wrote it for three groups in local policing agencies: (1) intelligence officers and analysts, (2) crime analysts who might need to use intelligence information and, (3) police managers who supervise crime and intelligence analysts. If you are such a manager, and you find that the work of analysts is something of a mystery, then we hope this manual can demystify their work and help you make better use of your analysts.

The coverage of this manual

The central focus of this manual is the analysis of data: making sense of the variety of bits of information describing criminal groups or problem gatherings. This manual does not cover:

- Federal, state, and local intelligence organizations, groups, and networks

- How to set up or manage an intelligence unit within a police organization

- All the sources of data and information available

- Security requirements for those with access to intelligence data

- Legal requirements for obtaining and sharing intelligence information

There are other documents, books, and resources that cover these topics.

Three key assumptions

1. In preparing to write this manual, it quickly became apparent that (1) there is considerable overlap in the analytic techniques employed and the skills needed by intelligence analysts and crime analysts and, (2) most police agencies would have insufficient resources to employ separate groups of both specialists. We have therefore assumed that intelligence analysis and crime analysis are broadly similar and will generally be undertaken by the same group of analysts.

2. In our early discussions with crime and intelligence analysts, they were able to identify only one important difference between their roles: That intelligence analysis focuses mainly on criminal groups and problem gatherings. Examples of the former would be terrorists, street gangs, outlaw motorcycle gangs, and organized shoplifters, and of the latter would be illegal street races, political demonstrations by extremist groups, and student crowds at spring break. Consequently, this manual focuses on analyzing information about criminal groups and problem gatherings.

3. The third assumption derives from our backgrounds in community policing and problem-oriented policing. The purpose of intelligence analysis should be to find ways of altering the "facilitating conditions" that permit these groups and gatherings to create harm. In other words, intelligence analysis can contribute both to long-term and immediate reductions in crime.

How is the manual organized?

The first part of the manual consists of 30 "Steps" organized under six sections. Each step covers a discrete topic and each one stands on its own. So there is no need to read the manual straight through from beginning to end; you can dip into it at any point. Nevertheless, topics do connect with each other and follow a logical order. Where these connections are vital, we reference other steps. At the end of most steps, we include some references to written materials that give more details about the topic.

The second part of the manual contains case studies of various criminal groups and problem gatherings that we undertook in order to assist our thinking about the uses of intelligence analysis. These case studies provide useful examples of the kinds of information that might be collected and ways in which it might be used.

Policing agencies and law enforcement

■ Throughout this manual, we use the term "police agencies" to refer to agencies of local government whose primary business is policing. As well as municipal and town agencies, this includes sheriff agencies that provide police services to county residents and businesses, but not those that only provide correctional, warrant, or court services. We do not include federal agencies, such as the Federal Bureau of Investigation (FBI), Drug Enforcement Administration (DEA), and Bureau of Alcohol, Tobacco, Firearms and Explosives (ATF).

■ We use the term "law enforcement" to refer to a procedure or tactic that police agencies can use, but we do not use the term "law enforcement agency" because law enforcement is only one of many tools police can use. Intelligence analysis should help police decision makers choose among the available tools.

READ MORE:

Jerry Ratcliffe. 2008. *Intelligence-Led Policing.*
Cullompton, Devon: Willan Publishing.

Ronald V. Clarke and John E. Eck. 2005. *Crime Analysis for Problem Solvers. In 60 Small Steps.* Washington, D.C.; U.S. Department of Justice, Office of Community Oriented Policing Services.

Part 1

Intelligence Analysis for Solving Problems

01

TERRORIST THREATS HAVE DRAWN ATTENTION TO THE VITAL ROLE OF INTELLIGENCE. However, the threats have also promoted inflated expectations and confusion regarding this role. This is particularly true in local policing. One source of confusion is that "intelligence" is used to refer both to raw information collected from some source and to the result of systematically analyzing this information. Many writings on intelligence analysis do little to clarify the term because they provide limited guidance as to what actions comprise analysis and the purposes these actions are supposed to serve.

National intelligence and criminal intelligence

While there are substantial differences between national intelligence (as conducted by federal agencies involved in international affairs) and criminal intelligence, we found Robert Clark's book (referenced below) on national intelligence helpful in defining the scope and objectives of police intelligence analysis. Clark asserts that intelligence analysis has five characteristics: orientation, target, goals, inputs, and methods. For policing, the first three characteristics are far more important and we discuss orientation, targets, and goals below.

Orientation – proactive

Intelligence analysis has a future orientation. It tries to determine what criminal activity is likely to happen if police do nothing to prevent it. In short, intelligence analysis is proactive. Consequently, reactive uses of information, such as to solve crimes that have already occurred, are not generally included in intelligence analysis. Solving crimes helps to redress past events, and though vital, this is not designed principally to prevent future incidents. Investigative information can be converted to intelligence when it is analyzed for the purpose of preventing future crimes.

Targets – groups

Intelligence analysis is directed against offenders operating in groups. Groups may facilitate offending, thus making them more serious than individual offenders acting alone. More importantly, intelligence can exploit the special vulnerabilities of groups, which are as follows:

- **Keeping Secrets.** Benjamin Franklin said, "Three can keep a secret if two are dead." While this is rather extreme, it illustrates an important point:

the more people who need to keep a secret, the less likely it is that the secret will be kept. This is why criminal groups often enforce secrecy with threats, and perhaps it is also the reason the Hell's Angels quote Benjamin Franklin. But, offender groups are not necessarily good at keeping their members compliant.

- **Visibility.** A related vulnerability is that the larger the group of offenders, the greater the difficulty of keeping a low profile. The danger is especially great when group members gather. Establishing secret meeting places helps them overcome this difficulty. But establishing such a place often requires group members to work with non-offenders (e.g., landlords) and this also increases their risk of detection. Groups that ostentatiously promote themselves create more information that intelligence analysis can exploit.

- **Coordination**. Unlike individual offenders operating alone, groups of offenders have to coordinate their activities with one another. Coordination difficulties rise as the group increases in size. Consequently, while groups have greater capacities than individuals, they are also less flexible, which, at least in the short run, makes them more predictable. In the long run, groups may have a greater chance to innovate than individuals, but this takes time.

In short, groups leak information that can be gathered and analyzed and, as we note below, the variety of information sources makes analysis mandatory.

Goal – prevention

The fundamental purpose of intelligence analysis is to prevent group crimes from occurring. This is consistent with the first two elements: a future orientation and group offending. Intelligence analysis targets groups in order to reduce crime. To serve this purpose, the detection, arrest, and prosecution of group offenders are important, but intelligence analysis is not limited to these actions. Going beyond law enforcement is critical to achieving crime reduction goals. Consistent with community and problem-oriented policing strategies, intelligence analysis can serve a wide range of preventive activities. In subsequent steps, we describe how intelligence analysis can expand the range of prevention activities by applying principles derived from environmental criminology.

Inputs – many

Intelligence analysis uses information from a wide variety of sources. It is not restricted to covert sources. Standard police records, available to the public, and other data collected by private and public agencies are often extremely useful. We examine some of the most obvious sources in this manual, but the sources available are only limited by imagination, resources, and technology. If intelligence analysis were restricted to a single source, the need for analysis would be much reduced. It is the need to make sense of multiple information sources, including data from other jurisdictions (see Step 22), each with its own strengths and weaknesses, that makes analysis important. Consequently, we do not define intelligence analysis by the type of information used: variety is what is important.

Methods – varied

Intelligence analysis methods involve processes to sort, interpret, and compare information from multiple sources in order to determine what offending groups are likely to be operating, how they commit crimes, and what can be done to keep these groups from being successful. Just as there are many sources of information, police can use many analytical methods. We will discuss some of the most important. We do not define intelligence analysis by the use of any particular method; any systematic approach that helps provide an accurate assessment can be part of intelligence analysis.

Lone wolves

What about the threat of "lone wolf" terrorists? Are their actions not susceptible to intelligence analysis? Practically speaking, no. Although the harm they can do is extreme, this does not mean that intelligence analysis can do any more for the lone wolf terrorist than it could do for the lone wolf bank robber, the isolated drug dealer, or the stand alone fraudster. If individual offending creates patterns, crime analysis can help. Controlling access to explosive materials, for example, helps thwart isolated terrorists as well as organized ones. However, without a group or a pattern of behavior, police have to rely on isolated and unpredictable reports of community members, chance encounters, and investigative work. This might happen when lone wolves "reach out" to others for assistance (e.g., obtaining weapons, information, or other support). When they mistakenly reach out to individuals with connections to police, this presents the police with an opportunity to identify and remove them.

In summary, *intelligence analysis is just a specialized form of crime analysis that focuses on problems created by groups of offenders.* It is a process for making sense of a diverse array of information about crime problems created by offender groups, with the goal of reducing crime. Intelligence is just a form of information that describes groups. Sources and methods do not define it.

READ MORE:

Robert M. Clark. 2007. *Intelligence Analysis: A Target-Centric Approach.* 2nd Edition. Washington, D.C.: CQ Press.

WE HAVE SAID THE GOAL OF INTELLIGENCE ANALYSIS IS TO REDUCE THE PROBLEMS CREATED BY OFFENDER GROUPS. Gathering, analyzing, and sharing data might assist in making arrests and prosecutions and could result in breaking up a group. However, this can only be considered effective action if the problems created by the group decline.

For example, breaking up a group that steals catalytic converters may not be productive, under the following circumstances:

1. The group was never responsible for an important proportion of the problem

2. The wrong members of the group are removed

3. Those arrested are quickly replaced by others, thus reestablishing the group

4. Other groups move in to take advantage of the now vacant opportunity

Unless there is a reduction of theft of catalytic converters, the actions were not effective. To ensure that they are effective, intelligence analysis should focus on the complete problem. In our example, the analysis should examine the catalytic converter theft process from beginning to end—from the characteristics of vehicles and victims to the reentry of the stolen converters into the legitimate market. In short, the problem is not the group stealing the catalytic converters, but the entire theft process, of which the group is an integral part.

These points can be illustrated by police attempts to disrupt street drug dealing, particularly in the late 1980s through the early 1990s when police targeted the most highly visible drug groups. Unfortunately, the most visible were not necessarily the most active in dealing or the most violent. In addition, informants sometimes directed police operations to serve their own needs; a difficulty that is made worse when there is little or no effort to gather systematic information on the problem so the informant's data can be evaluated in a larger context. Even when the group was a major contributor to the problem, the enforcement sometimes focused on those most easily replaced—retail dealers. Such easily replaced individuals are not critical to the functioning of the organizations.

Several randomized experiments conducted in the 1990s show the difference between an enforcement approach and an intelligence, problem-focused approach. (All these studies are reviewed in the National Research Council book referred to below.) First, let us consider Sherman and Rogan's experiment to determine the effectiveness of crack house raids in Kansas City. Possible raid targets were randomly allocated to receiving a raid and not receiving a raid. Though some crime reductions were observed at the raided houses relative to the other houses, these reductions were relatively minor.

Now, consider another experiment designed to look at the effectiveness of going beyond enforcement. In San Diego, Eck and Wartell looked at what happens if, after a raid, the landlord was compelled to improve apartment management practices. Raided addresses were randomly assigned to three groups: those that received no further treatment (control group); addresses where police sent the landlord a letter describing the raid and offering assistance (letter group); and addresses where police compelled the landlord to meet with narcotics detectives and city code inspectors and form a plan to improve the property (meeting group). All places had less drug dealing after the raid than before, but the meeting group places had a 60 percent reduction in crime relative to the control group (the letter group had outcomes between the control and meeting groups).

Finally, let us consider another drug experiment comparing problem-solving efforts at drug hot spots with enforcement crackdowns. Weisburd and Green randomly assigned street drug markets hot spots in Jersey City to either of these conditions. The problem solving approach showed far greater reductions in drug dealing and other forms of disorder than the standard enforcement approach.

These and other studies point to a consistent picture of the kinds of police strategies that work to reduce crime. In 2004, a National Research Council report described four policing strategies and their relative effectiveness (see Figure 1). The more focused the strategy and the wider array of tactics used, the more effective the strategy. In the lower left of Figure 1, the standard model of policing (relying predominately on random patrol, follow-up investigations, and rapid response) is the least effective strategy. It does not focus on specific places, people, or times and uses a predominately law enforcement approach.

Somewhat more effective is community policing (in the absence of problem solving). Community policing gains effectiveness by adding considerably more tactics, but it is still relatively unfocused. Focused policing, on the lower right in Figure 1, is far more effective than standard policing, because it narrows policing efforts to "hot" people, places, or times. Instead of spreading resources thinly, like standard policing, it concentrates resources. Intelligence analysis fits very well into this strategy. Evidence and theory suggest that combining the focus with a wider array of tactics improves police effectiveness more. That is the form of policing in the upper right part of Figure 1. The three experiments described above illustrate this point. All experiments involved focusing on hot places, but when police coupled law enforcement with other tactics they further increased their effectiveness at reducing crime and disorder.

The role of intelligence analysis in addressing problems is to shed light on how offenders behave so police can craft a solution. In short, intelligence analysis is an integral part of Problem-Oriented Policing. Often this will involve some sort of enforcement, but the enforcement will be highly targeted to have the greatest impact on the problem, and will often be part of a larger set of actions designed to make it harder for any remaining or new offenders to perpetuate the problem.

READ MORE:

National Research Council. 2004. *Fairness and Effectiveness in Policing.* Washington, D.C.: National Academies Press.

Figure 1. Policing strategy effectiveness

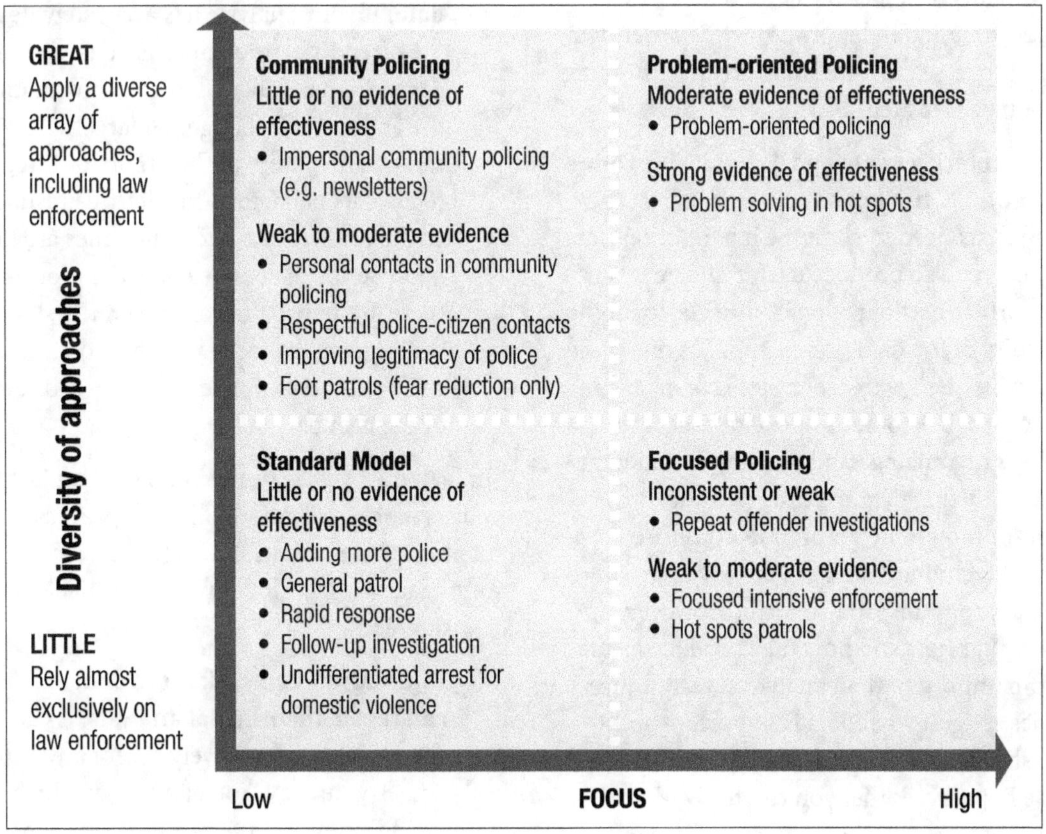

GREAT
Apply a diverse array of approaches, including law enforcement

Diversity of approaches

LITTLE
Rely almost exclusively on law enforcement

Community Policing
Little or no evidence of effectiveness
- Impersonal community policing (e.g. newsletters)

Weak to moderate evidence
- Personal contacts in community policing
- Respectful police-citizen contacts
- Improving legitimacy of police
- Foot patrols (fear reduction only)

Problem-oriented Policing
Moderate evidence of effectiveness
- Problem-oriented policing

Strong evidence of effectiveness
- Problem solving in hot spots

Standard Model
Little or no evidence of effectiveness
- Adding more police
- General patrol
- Rapid response
- Follow-up investigation
- Undifferentiated arrest for domestic violence

Focused Policing
Inconsistent or weak
- Repeat offender investigations

Weak to moderate evidence
- Focused intensive enforcement
- Hot spots patrols

Low   **FOCUS**   High

03

INTELLIGENCE ANALYSIS IS NOT SIMPLY THE COLLECTION OF COVERT DATA, nor is it making sure it is shared appropriately. Although collection and sharing receive considerable attention, and for very good reasons, this attention has obscured the simple fact that they are merely parts of a larger process illustrated by Figure 2. Our discussion of the process follows the numbered stages in the diagram.

1. **Targets create data.** Offender groups are the targets. Citizens might see them. They might act in ways that provoke police stops and arrests. They might write graffiti or create social network pages. They may have bank accounts. They may be recorded by closed circuit television (CCTV). In each of these examples, a person or machine captures data describing group members. In isolation and in these raw forms, these data are relatively meaningless.

2. **Police gather data.** Data from an informant, or on a digital recording device, or in a database needs to be collected to be analyzed. There are data capture processes that are obvious (e.g., police databases of offenders or CCTV footage from cameras near a crime site, confederates of members of an offender group) while other data capture processes require some creative thinking to recognize (see Steps 6–13).

3. **Analysts interpret data** and 4. **Analysts produce information**. Once police or others collect the data, analysts need to combine it with other data and interpret it to produce useful information. An important part of the analysis is determining the validity of the data (for example, is one piece of data consistent with other pieces of data from other sources). Another important aspect of analysis is organizing valid data into a coherent story. Organizing data requires analysts to use two sets of tools. One set of tools comprise analytical techniques: maps, network charts, statistical programs, and so forth. However, theories of groups and how they produce crime are more important than analytical techniques. Theories suggest what data is important and how it should fit with other data. Theories also provide hypotheses that you can test with the data (see Step 21). All good analysts have one

or more theories of how they can organize the data to produce a meaningful and valid story. We will discuss several such theories in later Steps 6 through 13. This analysis—with techniques and theories—creates information.

5. **Information helps police to decide what to do.** Information assists decision makers who choose actions. Decisions based on this information create actions whose purpose is to alter that target (for example, arresting members of the group) or the environment in which the target operates (for example, preventing group members from having access to key places, denying them weapons or other tools, or freezing their assets).

6. **Actions change the target and produce new data.** If your analysis has accurately described the offending group and its behaviors, and if the decision maker has used this information, then the actions will change the target. They may remove members of the group, or force the group to alter its behaviors. Ideally, this results in less crime or disorder. Such outcomes are known because the data emitted by the group changes—there are fewer attacks, less graffiti, less drug dealing, and so forth. The new data enters the cycle and helps police adjust their understanding of the group.

In fact, the cycle is more complex than just these six stages described. An intelligence process also consists of a series of feedback loops (2a, 3a, 5a) dependent on the target, information, and the decisions being considered.

■ 2a. **Analysts can seek more data** and 3a. **Analysts can revise their initial analysis.** As an analyst, you should not passively accept any data that comes your way. You can request the collection of additional data—for example asking that

Figure 2. Intelligence analysis process

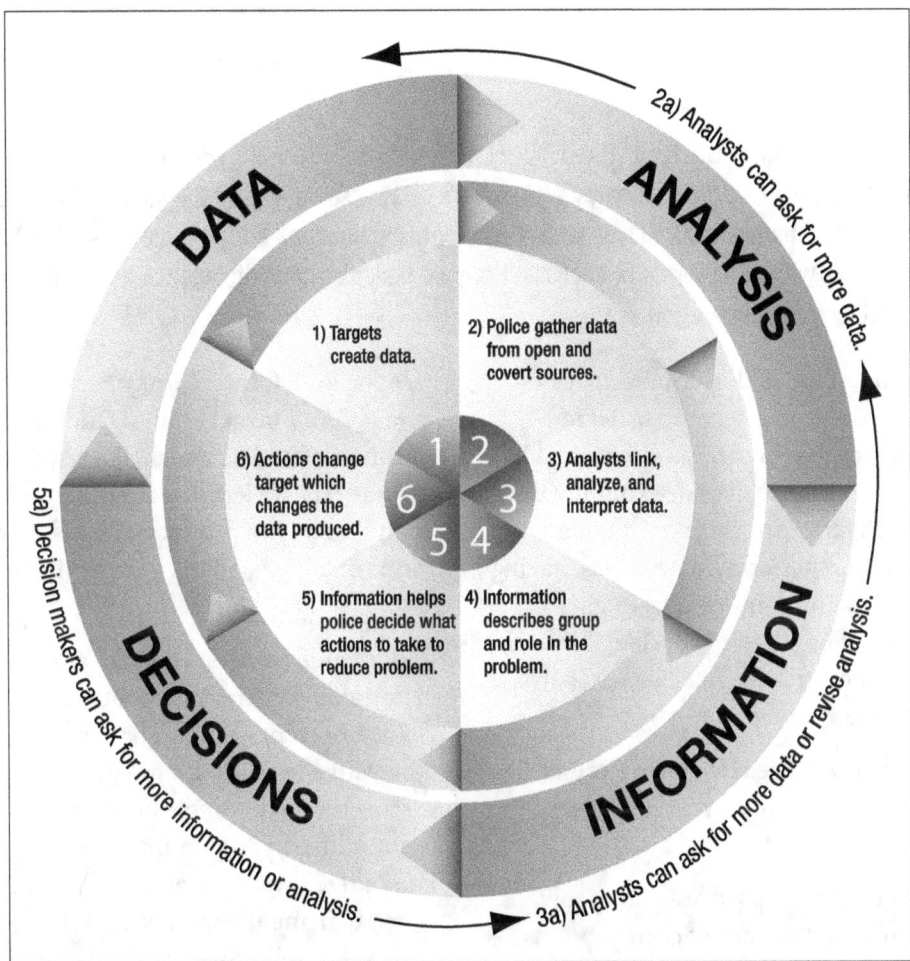

new questions be put to an informant. This new data might help test the reliability of previously collected data. It might fill in critical gaps about a group; it might be used to determine how the group makes use of its environment; or the new data may be needed to help determine which of several alternative hypotheses is more likely to be true (see Step 21). New data might require further analysis or the original analysis may have produced contradictory results so further analysis is needed, for example. The additional data would then have to be analyzed in light of the earlier information.

■ 5a. **Decision makers can ask for more information or analysis.** While decisions are being formulated you might be asked for additional information that could help refine the choice of actions. If the information is readily available, you can pass it on to other decision

makers. This might require going back further and conducting additional analysis. Or it might even require obtaining additional data.

The analysis process does not end with action against a target. You still need to determine if the actions had the desired effect. Does the group still exist? Have the group's criminal activities slowed down or stopped? Has the group changed its tactics to circumvent police actions? Have other groups moved in to replace the original group? Were there unintended consequences from the actions? Evaluating actions helps decision makers decide whether they should move on to other targets, make adjustments in how they handle this target, or whether their actions failed and they need to start over.

04

CRIME ANALYSTS USE THE TERM "ANALYSIS" TO REFER TO SPECIFIC TECHNIQUES THEY USE, SUCH AS GEOGRAPHIC analysis (i.e., crime mapping) or statistical analysis (to explore relationships among the variables in a data set). But the police use "analysis" in many other ways as well. This creates confusion about the meaning of the term and how "intelligence analysis" fits with other forms of analysis. Here we describe how intelligence analysis is related to other kinds of analysis used by local police agencies.

Perhaps the commonest use of the term by police relates to the type of decision it serves. **Strategic analysis** typically describes enquiries conducted to help long-term broad decisions—such as determining the appropriate approach for addressing repeat offenders. **Tactical analysis** serves shorter term decisions, having a narrower scope. So patrol commanders might ask for a tactical analysis of how best to allocate officers to handle a political demonstration. Intelligence analysis can be used at either level.

Analysis is also sometimes used by police to describe the "customers" for the analytical work, as in the following:

- **Investigative analysis** helps investigators solve particular crimes, or a pattern of crimes.

- **Patrol analysis** is designed to serve the needs of patrol officers and supervisors.

- **Traffic analysis** helps police focus resources on vehicle traffic (though sometimes the term is used to describe drug trafficking or communications traffic).

- **Problem analysis** is used by police and others involved in problem-oriented policing projects to reduce specific forms of crime and disorder.

A crime analysis unit may conduct any combination of these forms of analysis. As we will describe below, intelligence analysis overlaps investigative analysis and problem analysis.

Since crimes involve offenders, targets, and places, there can be analysis that focuses on all three of these elements. **Offender analysis** focuses on offenders, and is closely related to investigative analysis. In contrast, **place and geographic analysis** focuses on various geographic concentrations of crime—such as crime hot spots, repeat crime places, and risky facilities

(see the POP Center's *Risky Facilities Guide* for more details). And **target analysis** focuses on the people or things offenders attack. Forms of target analysis include repeat victim analysis, virtual repeat victim analysis, and hot product analysis. These and other forms of target analysis are used in problem analysis.

As shown in Figure 3 on page 17, target, place, and offender analysis overlap and all are forms of crime analysis (the examination of information to help prevent crime). For example, Joe Combs, a detective for the Cincinnati Police Department, discovered that a single apartment complex had an extraordinarily high number of burglaries (both compared to its previous history, and compared to other apartment complexes). Within the complex, several households were burgled multiple times, and most burglaries during this spike in crimes were committed by a small group of offenders (the burglaries declined following their arrest). He had discovered a combination of repeat places, repeat victimization, and repeat group offending.

It is useful to link forms of analysis to the types of problems the analysis is supposed to examine. That is why we define police intelligence analysis as focused on problems created by groups of offenders. Intelligence analysis is related to offender analysis (and investigative analysis) because of its focus on offender groups. Intelligence analysis also overlaps both place and target analysis. Consequently, intelligence analysis is a form of crime analysis as well.

Another way to see how intelligence analysis fits within crime analysis is to compare analysis used in reacting to crime patterns and those forms of analysis that attempt to understand the causes of crime patterns and to develop prevention initiatives. The first we will call reactive and the second proactive. We can also distinguish between analysis focusing on offenders and

Figure 3. Overlapping forms of crime analysis

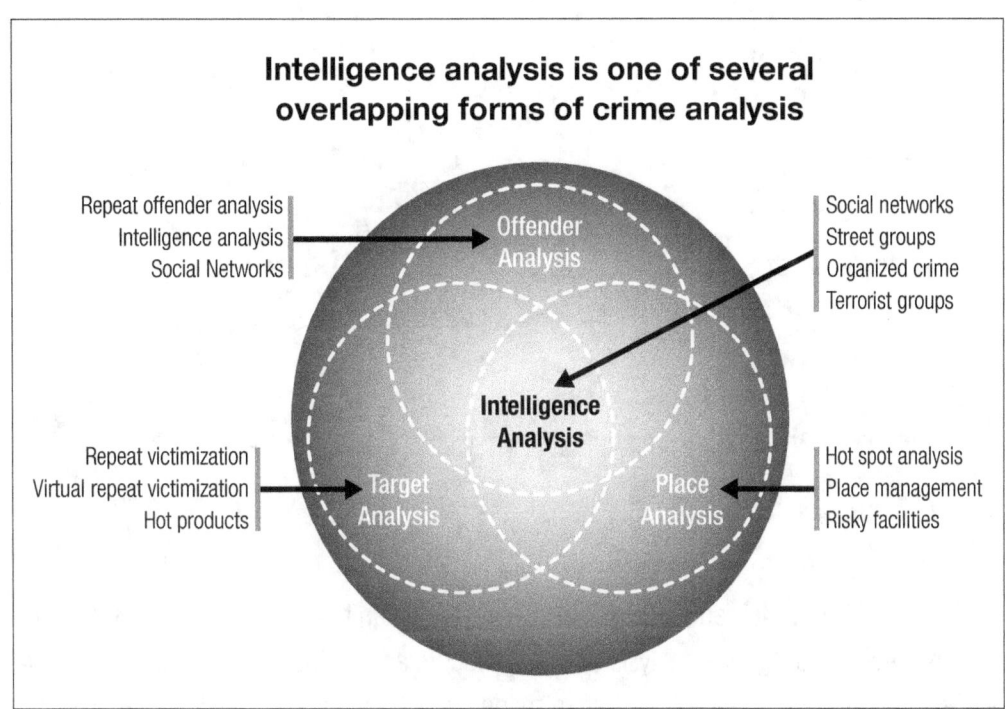

those focusing on crime patterns (such as geographic analysis). This gives us a simple way of organizing some of the most important forms of analysis (see Table 1). Intelligence analysis is a proactive form of offender analysis. It shares this proactive status with place analysis. Both place analysis and intelligence analysis are forms of problem analysis. Also, they stand in contrast to reactive analysis of crime patterns, such as simple hot spot detection and other forms of geographic analysis. This view of intelligence analysis underpins Jerry Ratcliffe's 3-i model, which portrays the role of intelligence analysis as an essential, action-oriented, decision support function (see *The 3-i Model* on page 18).

In conclusion, there is no standard way of classifying analysis types and many forms of analysis overlap. Intelligence analysis shares many features with many types of crime analysis. We believe that the distinguishing feature of intelligence analysis concerns not techniques but the fact that intelligence analysis focuses attention on offender groups.

Table 1. Reactive and proactive forms of crime analysis

REACTIVE AND PROACTIVE FORMS OF CRIME ANALYSIS		
	Reactive	Proactive
Offenders	Investigative analysis – the analyst examines databases to assist investigators solve a crime or crime series.	Intelligence analysis – the analyst pulls together information on problems created by offender groups to help craft methods for reducing that problem.
Locations	Patrol analysis – the analyst examines databases to help determine when and where police should allocate patrol resources.	Place-analysis – the analyst pulls together information from databases, targeted information gathering and other sources to reduce problems at particular locations.

The 3-i model

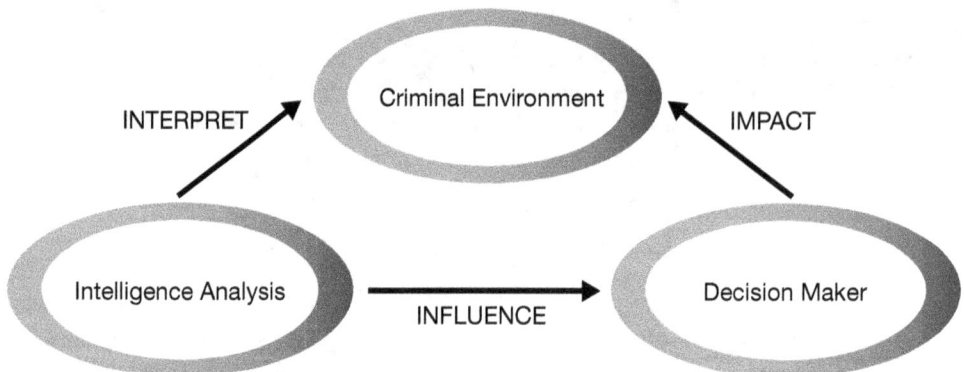

Jerry Ratcliffe's **3-i model** redefines the role of analysis in an intelligence-led policing environment. Instead of viewing intelligence analysis as simply understanding the criminal environment, the **3-i model** demands that intelligence analysts also identify decision makers and influence their thinking. Decision makers are people who have the power and resources to have an impact on the criminal environment. Thus, intelligence analysts have a leadership role within policing, guiding priorities, and resource decisions.

Ratcliffe's **3-i model** begins with an arrow from analysis to the criminal environment. This emphasis is deliberate. Analysts can't wait for data to come to them: they have to actively seek out the information they need. Creating and disseminating an intelligence product is not a sufficient outcome in the **3-i model**. Instead analysts must identify a decision-making framework they can influence and actively work to help decision makers have a direct impact on the criminal environment. Making recommendations to guide decision makers (both inside and outside policing) to prevent, disrupt or reduce criminal activity is a vital role of the analyst. Learning the theory and practice of what works to reduce crime is crucial.

Ratcliffe's **3-i model** challenges analysts and decision makers to work closely together. It rethinks the role of intelligence analysis as an essential, action-oriented, decision support function.

Source: Ratcliffe, J. H. (2008) Intelligence-Led Policing, Willan Publishing. For further information see www.jratcliffe.net.

AS MENTIONED IN STEP 2, IN 2004 THE NATIONAL RESEARCH COUNCIL PUBLISHED A COMPREHENSIVE ASSESSMENT of police research and policy. It showed how all policing strategies fall into four groups, depending on the degree to which they focus on specific crime problems and the range of tactics they employ. These four groups are standard policing, community policing, focused policing, and problem-oriented policing (see Table 2). Intelligence analysis plays somewhat different roles in each strategy.

Standard policing makes the least use of intelligence analysis. Standard policing is relatively unfocused and employs a limited number of law enforcement tactics generically across a wide variety of circumstances. The principal tactics are patrolling, reactive follow-up investigations, and rapid response to calls. To improve effectiveness, the main approach is to add more police and do more of the same. Research has shown that at best this has very limited effects on crime, fear of crime, or disorder. Standard policing uses very little information and makes little use of crime analysis to assist in making critical decisions. Intelligence analysis, when used, is the province of highly specialized units that often communicate poorly with standard patrol operations.

Standard policing is ineffective for several reasons. First, it does not use information to focus resources on the relatively few people, places, and circumstances that need the most attention. Consequently, it spreads its resources too thin where they are most needed. Further, the lack of information makes it difficult to develop

innovative tactics that exploit the vulnerabilities of offenders. Finally, standard policing puts more emphasis on following routine law enforcement and arrest practices than on preventing crime.

Community policing seeks to bridge the gap between police and community. It places far less emphasis on law enforcement and uses a wider repertoire of policing tactics. However, community policing is relatively unfocused unless it includes a strong component of problem solving. Research evidence suggests that it can be somewhat more effective at reducing crime than standard policing, but the results are ambiguous. Like standard policing, most community policing makes limited use of information technology, crime analysis, and intelligence.

The strength of community policing is that it provides the foundation for the two-way exchange of information between members of the public and the police. This is particularly critical in neighborhoods suffering from high levels of crime and when dealing with crime groups hidden within communities, or

Table 2. Intelligence in policing strategies

	LOW FOCUS	HIGH FOCUS
Limited tactics Mostly Law Enforcement	Standard policing Very little influence on crime Very little use of intelligence analysis	Focused policing Strong influence on crime Intelligence data from limited sources which is used to target enforcement on crime groups
Wide variety of tactics Including Some Law Enforcement	Community policing Modest influence on crime Improves the flow of intelligence data from community members	Problem-oriented policing Highly effective against crime Intelligence from variety of sources is used to craft interventions that curtail crime group activities

intimidating community members. In the absence of community policing, developing intelligence on these groups can be extremely difficult. For these reasons community policing is a necessary condition for effective intelligence analysis. It is a foundation strategy on which other strategies can be built.

Focused policing strategies are a collection of approaches that build on the law enforcement tactics used in standard policing by making much greater use of information. Information is used to identify offenders and places that are disproportionately involved in crime. There is strong evidence that targeting very high crime *places* can reduce crime considerably, but evidence about the usefulness of targeting persistent *offenders* is much less clear. This can increase the chances of arresting the most prolific offenders, but existing studies have failed to examine whether crime declined as a result of such targeting.

Because focused policing places information analysis at the forefront of policing, intelligence is more important for this strategy than for the standard policing or community policing. However, in the absence of community support, only limited intelligence is available. Furthermore, when limited to law enforcement tactics, focused policing does not address the facilitating conditions that allow criminal groups to operate. So focused policing, like community policing, is a foundation for effective use of intelligence. But neither is sufficient on its own and we need to combine community and focus.

Problem-oriented policing, which was developed to address the limitations of standard policing, succeeds in combing community and focus.

It was specifically designed to be highly focused—thus capturing the advantages of focused policing—and to use a variety of tactics with the community—thus building on community policing. It addresses any and all aspects of crimes, including the places involved, the targets and victims affected, and the offenders.

Research into problem-oriented policing practices has shown that it is highly effective at reducing crime and disorder. Though there are few head-to-head comparisons between focused policing and problem-oriented policing, the research that is available shows that following a problem-oriented approach has greater benefits than simply focusing on crime hotspots.

The basic principles of problem-oriented policing are simple to state. First, problem-oriented policing places far greater emphasis on what the police are to accomplish—the ends of policing—than on the means of policing. As long as the policing practices are constitutional and legal, are acceptable to the community, are affordable, and have a high likelihood of being effective, problem-oriented policing does not specify what should be done. Instead, problem-oriented policing states that the goals of police are to reduce community problems. Second, problem-oriented policing claims that information needs to be examined to determine how specific problems arise and to determine what sorts of actions can be done to reduce or eliminate these problems. Third, problem-oriented policing calls for a thorough search for solutions to the problem, not limited to law enforcement options. Finally, since the goal of problem solving is to solve the problem, problem-oriented policing requires evaluation of the outcomes of the intervention.

These principles have been codified in the well-known SARA process (see Figure 4). SARA stands for Scanning, Analysis, Response, and Assessment. This is a cyclical model that starts with the identification and definition of a problem (Scanning), followed by detailed analysis (Analysis). Intelligence analysts can play important roles at these initial stages by helping to identify groups that are generating serious crime problems and producing information that describes how they operate. Response is the third stage, where solutions are developed and implemented. Intelligence analysis can help identify possible interventions based on information describing group vulnerabilities.

The last stage (Assessment) is the evaluation of the intervention. Again, intelligence analysis can help determine if the interventions worked by looking at the impact on the targeted group and whether their crimes have declined. In Figure 4, the large clockwise arrows show the standard cycle. The smaller, inner arrows indicate that often a problem-solving process needs to revisit earlier stages as new questions arise or evidence suggests that interventions are not working as expected.

READ MORE:

David Weisburd and John Eck. 2004. "What Can Police Do to Reduce Crime, Disorder and Fear?" *The Annals of the American Academy of Political and Social Science* 593:42–65.

Figure 4. Stages of the SARA process

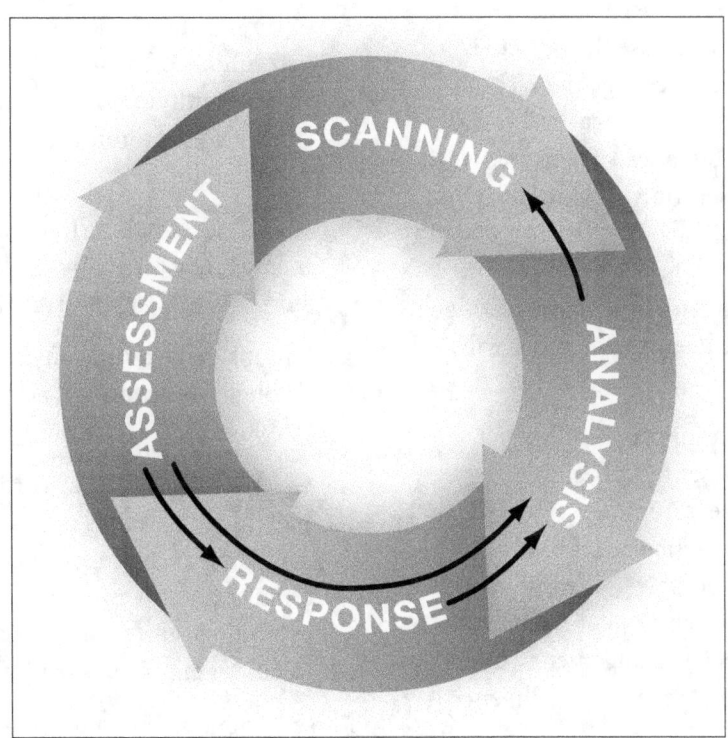

06

A USEFUL STARTING POINT FOR APPROACHING INTELLIGENCE ANALYSIS is to assume that offenders choose to take advantage of limited crime opportunities. They take advantage of situations where crime is easy, low risk, rewarding, socially encouraged, or provoked. There is considerable evidence that focusing on offender choices can reduce crime, and there are many ways to address crime by blocking opportunities.

"Choice" means that offenders select actions they think will help them achieve their purposes. In making these choices, offenders have limited and sometimes confusing information. They also often have limited time and competing objectives. To address these limits, they use rules of thumb and habit to reduce the information they need and to increase the speed of their decisions. "Do what others in my group do," is one such rule of thumb. "Do what worked before," is another such rule.

Understanding offender choice is critical to intelligence analysis. This is because the principle method of reducing crime is to change these choices. We do this by manipulating the physical and social environment surrounding offenders. There are five choice criteria offenders use: effort, risk, reward, excuses, and provocations. The less effort or risk, the greater the likelihood the offender will commit a crime. The more reward, greater the excuses, or higher the provocations, the more likely the offender will choose crime.

These five criteria influence all people—not just offenders—in all choices—not just offending. Features of the immediate environment signal the individual as to whether a particular set of actions will be useful or counterproductive. The individual then makes a choice. This environment includes the physical setting and the social arrangements. One very important social environment for intelligence is the offenders' group.

An offender in a group may make a very different choice than the same offender outside a group but facing the same circumstances. Groups provide a context that influences individual choice (see Table 3 on page 23):

1. Group members can make crime **easier** by supplying tools, providing transportation, sharing information, and taking on some of the work. A crime that one person cannot do, may be feasible with a group.

2. Groups can make it **safer** (fewer risks) by mutual protection and sharing information about possible risks. Identifying suspects may become harder if witnesses cannot distinguish among several confederates.

3. Groups also make crime **excusable** for their members by justifying the behavior and providing stories as to why the crime is "really necessary."

4. Groups make crime **enticing** to their members through peer pressure, and by providing examples to follow.

5. Groups make crime **rewarding** by giving individual members a sense of belonging, providing an audience to celebrate successful crimes, and other intangible, but important, psychological rewards, in addition to the more familiar tangible rewards of crime.

These attributes, which we collectively call **ESEER**, correspond to standard choice criteria we all use when selecting actions: effort, risk, excuses, provocations, and rewards. These are so critical to understanding crime and its prevention, we will return to them repeatedly throughout this manual.

To an outsider, considering the individual offender in the abstract, the choice may seem inexplicable and even irrational. When examined in the context of a group of offenders, the same choice appears reasonable (even though objectionable). However, groups do not inevitably increase crime. Offender groups can control their members' behaviors so that individuals only choose crimes when it is more likely to aid the group. As we will discuss later (Step 26), it is sometimes possible to exploit the group to reduce offending.

Because individuals seldom have complete knowledge about other members of their group, they may misinterpret the circumstances. One example is called "pluralistic ignorance." This describes circumstances where each member of a group believes other members value something when in fact few if any other members actually value it. However, to please the others, each group member professes that they too hold that value, thus justifying what the others believed. As a result, the group members express a preference that no individual alone would prefer. Within an offender group, no individual may want to get involved in a fight with another group, but thinking that the other members do want to get into a fight, and believing they will lose face if they refuse, all members of the group jump into the fight.

A commonly held misconception is that people in large crowds lose their self-identity and become "irrational." However, considerable research on crowds shows that this is not the case. People make choices in crowds just as they do outside of crowds. The difference is that within a crowd, an individual will also take into account what other people are doing and what is happening to them. From an outsider's perspective, the crowd may seem as a single entity that transcends the individuals that make it up. However, from inside it is clear that a crowd, of any size, comprises individuals and small groups, often with very different interests. Intelligence analysis can play an important role in helping to maintain orderly crowds by providing information on the diversity of interests within a crowd and helping to separate the few troublemakers from the many other individuals.

While offenders take advantage of existing opportunities for crime, they can also manipulate situations to extend opportunities and make new ones. An organized crime group that bribes a local politician creates opportunities for taking public funds. A terrorist group that infiltrates a member into security forces opens up opportunities for further terrorist activities that did not exist before. Street gang intimidation of witnesses expands the ability of the gang to engage in criminal activity. Intelligence analysis should look at how offending groups manipulate their environments to extend their opportunities.

READ MORE:

Ronald Clarke. 2008. "Situational Crime Prevention." In *Environmental Criminology and Crime Analysis*, ed. Richard Wortley and Lorraine Mazerolle. Cullompton, Devon: Willan Publishing.

Table 3. How groups influence choices

CHOICE CRITERIA	INFLUENCE OF GROUP	EXAMPLES
Effort	Makes crime **easier**	Dividing a complex task or spreading effort among several offenders
Risks	Makes crime **safer**	Providing protection, sharing information, or intimidating witnesses
Excuses	Makes crime more **excusable**	Claiming crimes are permissible or desirable, and denigrating victims
Provocations	Makes crime more **enticing**	Pressuring, encouraging, or guiding members
Rewards	Makes crime more **rewarding**	Providing an audience, status, and reputation

THE MOST ESSENTIAL REQUIREMENT FOR CRIME IS OPPORTUNITY. Regardless of a person's motivations, if there is no opportunity there can be no crime. Further, a tempting opportunity may entice a person to commit a crime they would not ordinarily consider. Offender groups can develop to exploit specific opportunities. Human traffickers and smugglers take advantage of two opportunities: the desire of people to leave impoverished countries and the demand for cheap human labor in other countries. Internet commerce created the opportunities that cyber gangs exploit. Drunken bar patrons provide opportunities for youth groups to commit robberies.

Opportunities are situations that offenders can exploit for their gain (e.g., material reward, social dominance, revenge, relief from threat, and so forth). The basic structure of opportunities is often depicted by the problem analysis triangles (see Figure 5). The inner triangle shows the three elements required for a crime to occur: a ready **offender** or group of offenders, a desirable **target** (person, animal, or thing), and a **place** for the two to interact. At minimum, crime opportunities occur when offenders are at places with desirable targets. Removing any one of these three required elements can eliminate the opportunity. Standard law enforcement focuses on offender removal. This can be useful, if the offenders are not easily replaced (Step 13), but there are other ways to reduce crime that also must be considered, either for use with enforcement or as stand-alone options.

Figure 5. The problem analysis triangles

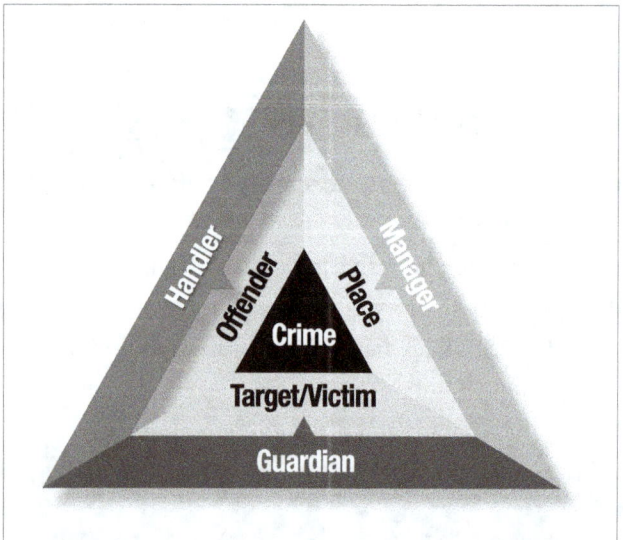

There is more to crime opportunities than these three basic elements: a crime opportunity also requires absence or ineffectiveness of any of the three outer elements of the triangle.

■ **Guardians** are people who protect the target—owners of things the offender wants to take or damage, friends of people the offender would like to attack, or security guards hired to protect buildings from terrorist attack.

■ **Handlers** are people who try to keep the potential offender out of trouble. They can be parents, siblings, spouses, friends, coworkers, teachers, clergy, and others with whom the potential offender is positively socially connected. They can even be other offenders.

■ Finally, **managers** are people who control spaces: owners of locations (private or public), hired employees who work at the location, or others to whom the owner has delegated authority to regulate conduct at the place.

Collectively, we call handlers, guardians, and managers **controllers**, as they control their corresponding elements on the inner triangle. Consequently, in addition to removing one or more of the inner elements, adding one or more controllers helps to reduce crime.

The convergence of offenders with targets at accessible places, in the absence of controllers, makes crime possible. When this happens repeatedly, a crime pattern emerges. Why does this occur? The normal routines of everyday life create most crime opportunities. These include commuting and school schedules. Street drug dealers often locate near commuter routes and when they do so their daily activity patterns follow the routines of commuters

Intelligence Analysis for Problem Solvers

and students. Armed robbery groups can exploit the regular patrons of entertainment districts and drinking routines. The routines of the internet allow fraudsters to exploit users. Natural disasters disrupt some routines, but create other routines that offenders can exploit, including the routines of insurance companies and government aid agencies. Car and suicide bombings by terrorist groups are feasible because people routinely gather at particular places: markets, hotels, and transportation hubs, for example. A peaceful political march creates a routine that small groups of offenders can exploit to create disturbances. Driving routines leave some stretches of highway largely vacant for periods, thus allowing street racing groups to use them. Knowing the spatial and temporal patterns of crime is not just important for allocating law enforcement, it is critical for identifying the routines the crime group is exploiting so that sustainable prevention can be introduced.

Opportunity is in the eye of the offender. Offenders, singly or in groups, judge reward, effort, risk, excuses, and provocations (see ESEER in Step 6) by the presence and absence of the six elements described by the problem triangle. The presence of a target at a place reduces effort while suggesting reward and perhaps providing a provocation. Guardians and managers influence risk and effort. Other offenders can increase excuses and provocations as well as reduce effort and risk. Handlers reduce excuses and provocations, and sometimes rewards.

Offenders, however, can manipulate situations to increase the crime opportunities. Manipulation of opportunities—creating new ones or improving existing ones—is easier for offenders in groups than those operating singly.

Targets and their guardians

Groups enhance the ability of offenders to manipulate targets. A group of offenders has an easier time finding targets because they have more people looking. Sheer numbers can overwhelm a target's defenses and overcome guardians. A group of offenders has greater ability to intimidate victims, thus reducing the chances of effective police involvement. Specialization within a group allows it to undertake complex offenses, from con games to terrorist attacks. A large group, with sufficient resources, can bribe guardians to gain access to targets. Similarly, it can infiltrate a legitimate organization.

Offenders and their handlers

Groups promote offending through recruitment of members and allies. A large group can isolate its members, thus reducing outside influences—such as from parents—and increasing the influence of other group members. In this way, they replace outside handlers with inside handlers. Groups can also promote offender learning. Members of the group learn about what works and what does not to successfully pull off a crime. This information can be disseminated throughout the group and passed down to future members. Importantly, groups produce both excuses and provocations for committing crimes. However, in some circumstances you may be able to take advantage of how offenders in groups handle each other to reduce group violence (Step 26).

Places and their managers

Offender groups can seize control of places that an individual offender cannot. A drug-dealing group can hold a street corner against other dealers more easily than a dealer can on his own, for example. Terrorist organizations in some countries hold large swaths of territory. Offender groups can use places for meetings; for stashing weapons, drugs, and other goods; for prostitution and other human exploitation; for safe houses; and other purposes. Whether seized or purchased, once a place is controlled by the group it can organize the physical space to facilitate its activities. These methods can result in reduced risk or effort, or increased rewards.

Even if the group does not completely take over a location, they can bribe, intimidate, or replace managers so that the group can be sure that the place operates in a manner that helps their activities.

READ MORE:

Marcus Felson. 2008. "Routine Activity Theory." In *Environmental Criminology and Crime Analysis,* ed. Richard Wortley and Lorraine Mazerolle. Cullompton, Devon: Willan Publishing.

Marcus Felson and Ronald V. Clarke. 1998. *Opportunity Makes the Thief.* Police Research Series Paper 98. London: Home Office.

YOU SHOULD DISTINGUISH CRIMINAL GROUPS (such as pedophile rings and outlaw motorcycle gangs) from problem gatherings (such as juveniles involved in cruising or who meet for street racing). In both cases, you need to analyze the conditions that permit them to operate in your jurisdiction and ultimately work to remove these conditions. An important distinction between groups and gatherings concerns their internal structure:

■ Groups are composed of offenders connected by some form of internal structure. Examples of structure include routine communications links, hierarchy, chains of command, and recruitment and expulsion practices. These and other forms of structure can be clear, strong, and enduring (area C in Figure 6), but often they are vague, weak, and transitory (Step 9).

■ Gatherings are collections of individuals at particular places and time. Gatherings have little or no structure. Many gatherings are only collections at a place and time of separate individuals with no other connections (area A), but some gatherings have weak internal structures, thus overlapping with groups (area B). Typically, many participants have no intent to offend.

Here are three examples illustrating these distinctions:

1. A local bus system efficiently transports students to and from their schools by routing busses through a downtown hub where passengers can transfer. Students from many different schools congregate at the transit hub. If there are no other connections among the students, this is an example of a gathering. Within this gathering, a few individual students may bully and steal from other students, but they do not coordinate their activities in any way. Some of the non-offending students, nevertheless, may provide cover for the offenders. Here, the environment (the school, bus systems, the transit hub, gathering of students) provides an external structure and a set of crime opportunities for individual offenders.

2. Some youths from the same school may travel together so they can intimidate and steal from other students at the transit hub. They target students from a rival school waiting for particular busses at particular times. Here we see the overlap of gathering and group: the offending students have a rudimentary internal structure that helps them exploit their environment, but the environment is still providing most of the structure.

3. A neighborhood street gang robs pedestrians and runs a protection racket for merchants. It has a leader, rules for entry and conduct, and a hierarchy. Members use vehicles to get around and find likely targets. The internal structure here is strong, and allows the group to make use of the environment. Further, the group members can manipulate the environment to further their criminal activities. For example, they may alter the physical environment by using a meeting place and adapting it to their use (e.g., destroying streetlights). Intimidation alters the social environment to reduce their risks of apprehension.

Figure 6. Groups and gatherings

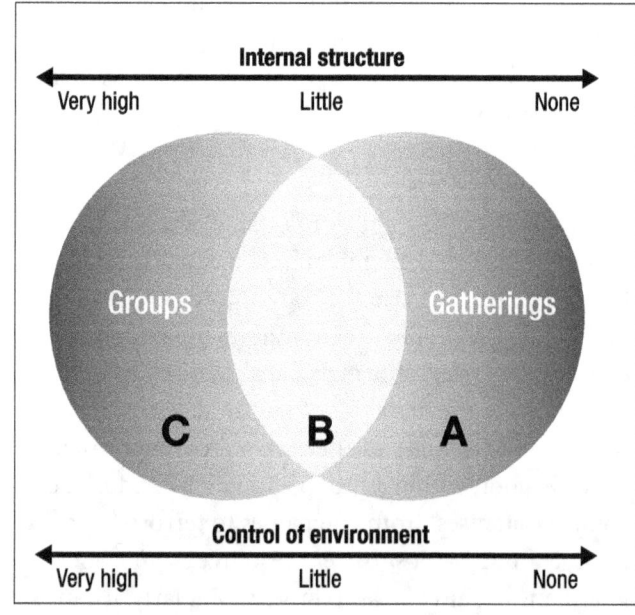

While participants in a gathering are extremely dependent on the physical and social environment, members of a criminal group use their internal structure to control their environment. Internal structure can protect a group's core members from the physical and social environment within which it operates. This means that leaders of criminal groups are exposed to fewer risks from the police and from rival groups. The downside of a group organization is that it is costly—senior members need to compensate junior members and others for the risks they run. Further, as groups become more organized they are likely to grow, and the larger they become, the greater attention they attract from the police. Finally, a tightly organized criminal group is less flexible in adapting to changes in the environment.

Sometimes it will be difficult for you to determine if you are dealing with an organized group or an unstructured gathering. If individual offenders perceive the physical and social environment in the same way, these offenders may behave in the same way and appear more organized than they really are. Here are some hypothetical examples of how this confusion can arise:

■ Copper thieves can independently learn that vacant buildings in a particular neighborhood are good targets. Here thieves take advantage of the environment provided. Since each thief sees the same environment, each behaves the same way, even though they are not coordinating their actions. In contrast, an owner of a recycling business might recruit thieves, direct them to vulnerable targets, provide transportation, settle disputes among thieves, and provide guarantees that they are paid. In this case, the owner is creating an organization that is not completely dependent on the environment. To you, the two scenarios may look the same. You could mistakenly believe that in the first instance the thefts were organized or in the second instance that the thieves were disorganized individuals merely taking advantage of an obvious opportunity. Your intelligence analysis can help avoid such mistakes.

■ Speeding may be highly concentrated along a particular stretch of highway at particular times, because each driver perceives the same opportunity to speed. Drivers only take into account the road in front of them and the cars in their immediate vicinity, but do not follow instructions from a "head" driver. The stable environment creates recurrent patterns of congestion and speeding. Intelligence analysis is not helpful with such collections (though crime analysis is). Let us contrast this speeding example to illegal road racing. An illegal road-racing gathering needs some organization, but not much because the relevant environment—the street system—is highly predictable and well understood by its members. Members know that on certain nights, particular stretches of road will be highly suitable for racing. The gathering only needs to be organized enough for members to know that others will show up at advantageous times and places and will obey the same rules of conduct. Such a gathering can operate because the environment provides much of the information necessary to coordinate activities. Such a group is highly dependent on this environment—if it changes then the group may have difficulty adapting. Nevertheless, a rudimentary organization facilitates the races.

■ A group must be organized if it is to export stolen cars on a routine basis. The environment still produces opportunities (e.g., being near a port city), but to select the types of vehicles the export market wants, in the volume necessary, and coordinate the thefts with the shipping, the offenders must be far more organized than the street racers. Though these offenders are exercising more control over their environment, changes in the environment (e.g., tighter controls over who is allowed into the port facilities) can reduce the ability of this organization to function.

You can reduce the ability of organized groups to commit crimes by breaking them up or by changing the physical or social environment on which they rely. The importance of these two approaches will vary by the internal structure of the organization you are analyzing. The rare extremely organized crime groups will require far more law enforcement effort, though changing the environments can help undermine their capabilities. The more frequently encountered loosely structured organizations will be more vulnerable to environmental changes and less responsive to enforcement. Problematic gatherings, being more dependent on their environments, are best addressed by altering these environments.

09

THE POPULAR IMAGE OF "ORGANIZED CRIME" IS THAT OF LARGE, ENDURING MAFIA-TYPE SYNDICATES, often with international reach, which are involved in a variety of criminal enterprises including extortion, racketeering, drug sales, and human trafficking. These syndicates have strict hierarchies of authority and demand extreme loyalty from their members, who might perform specialist roles. When necessary, they will seek to corrupt officials and they will use violence to enforce obedience from those they exploit or victimize.

While such organizations still exist, their prominence has faded and they now comprise only a minority of organized criminal groups. Far more common are small, organized networks of entrepreneurial offenders, often transitory in nature, that develop to exploit particular opportunities for illegal profit. These groups vary from temporary associations created to commit a time-limited series of offenses, to enduring businesses that invest in on-going criminal activities (see Table 4).

The formal definitions of organized crime recently adopted by the national police forces in the U.K. and Germany, as well as by the European Union, reflect this new reality. In all cases, the definitions try to include the entrepreneurial groups, principally by stating that the organized group can be composed of as few as two individuals. For example, the German federal crime intelligence office, the Bundeskriminalamt (or BKA), defines organized crime as follows:

"The planned violation of the law for profit or to acquire power, where offences are each, or together, of a major significance, and are carried out by more than two participants who co-operate within a division of labor for a long or undetermined time span using: a) commercial or commercial-like structures, or b) violence or other means of intimidation, or c) influence on politics, media, public administration, justice and legitimate economy."

Many of the crimes committed by organized criminals—for example; human smuggling, drug trafficking, sex trafficking, and money laundering—depend on overseas contacts. Opportunities for these crimes have expanded in line with increased globalization and developments in technology.

Thus, the growth in international trade has made it easier to import drugs and to export stolen motor vehicles. The rise of the Internet and cell phone technology has made it easier to coordinate transnational crimes. The expansion of air travel has facilitated migration, legal and illegal, which brings with it increased opportunities for crime.

Table 4. Types of criminals

ORGANIZED CRIME SYNDICATES	NETWORKS OF CRIMINAL ENTREPRENEURS
Few in number	Many
Large	Small
Regional/national	Local
Stable, enduring	Unstable, temporary
Outside normal society	Integrated in society
Structured	Loosely knit
Hierarchical	"Flat" organization
Static membership	Fluid membership
Differentiated roles	Undifferentiated roles
Entrenched leadership	Changing leadership
Formal rules/regulations	Informal agreements
Criminal identity	Business identity
Full-time illegal operations	Part-time operations
Ties of loyalty	Business relationships
Use of violence	Avoidance of violence
Crime generalists	Crime specialists
Abundant resources	Limited resources
Sophisticated technology	Everyday technology
Seek opportunities	Respond to opportunities

Source: Bullock, Tilley, and Clarke 2010.

This is because recent immigrants still have ties in their home countries, which enable those so inclined to find the partners needed for transnational crime.

Given the wider definition of organized criminal groups, it is likely that several such groups, involved in quite different crimes, might independently be operating within your jurisdiction. One group might be specializing in home invasions, another in carjacking, a third in sex trafficking, and so forth. This considerably complicates the role of your department in respect of organized crimes and also provides difficult challenges for you in helping your police colleagues deal with the groups.

The purposes of intervention

In subsequent steps of the manual, we discuss in detail a number of organized groups. We will show that each group is different, that you must acquire different data about each one, and you will need to create tailor-made interventions. The purpose of intervening will vary with the nature of the group, as follows:

1. Some of the criminal groups, terrorist cells for example, are so dangerous that the principal objective of police action must be to remove them—i.e., identify and arrest the group members as soon as possible. As in the case of terrorists, this task would often be handed over to the federal authorities.

2. In many other cases, say an organized burglary ring, the prime responsibility for identifying and arresting the group would fall to your department, using largely the same approach when identifying and arresting individual criminals.

3. In a third group of cases, taking out the group might not be realistic or even particularly desirable. In dealing with street gangs, for example, the principal objective will usually be to restrict their capacity, or opportunity, to engage in behavior that is harmful to them or to the community. In other words, when dealing with organized groups, local police will often be involved in preventive action.

4. Even when the primary objective is to identify and arrest a dangerous group, an important additional objective should always be to prevent the formation of new groups to take the place of

those arrested. Essentially, this involves applying principles of situational crime prevention to identify and modify the opportunities, or "facilitating conditions," favorable to the formation or operation of these groups. This task, discussed in the next step, puts intelligence analysts in a central role.

Marcus Felson has applied his routine activity theory to develop the following *"Rules for Understanding and Reducing Organized Crimes"*

1. Divide organized crimes into very specific types.
2. Focus on the acts, not the group engaged in them.
3. Expect considerable variation among groups in organization.
4. Assume that such crime is seldom ingenious.
5. Monitor and thwart the opportunity for small-time crime
6. Closely study the *modus operandi* in committing the crimes
7. Find out how crime feeds off legitimate and marginal activities.
8. Tease out the sequence of events for ongoing criminal cooperation.
9. Interfere with that sequence, access to the customer, or *modus operandi.*
10. Use situational prevention to reduce crime opportunities that feed organized crime, directly and indirectly.

Adapted from: Felson 2006

READ MORE:

Karen Bullock, Ronald V. Clarke, and Nick J. Tilley. 2010. *Situational Prevention of Organized Crimes.* Cullompton, Devon: Willan Publishing.

Marcus Felson. 2006. *The Ecosystem for Organized Crime,* United Nations European Institute for Crime Prevention and Control (HEUNI), Paper No. 26.

10

THE FACILITATING CONDITIONS THAT ALLOW A PARTICULAR ORGANIZED GROUP TO FORM AND OPERATE include both the physical conditions of the immediate situations in which the offenses occur and the wider social arrangements that make the crime possible. We can illustrate these by assuming that your jurisdiction harbors a group involved in stealing cars for export. Some of the facilitating conditions in your jurisdiction might include the following:

1. You are close to the Mexican border, to a deep-water port, or to a ferry terminal that serves Caribbean or South American countries.

2. You have substantial immigrant communities with ties to these countries, or temporary immigrant workers from these countries.

3. Local businesses trade with these countries.

4. The SUVs and pick-ups favored by local residents fetch high prices in these countries.

5. Young immigrant men have been thrown out of work by the recession and have become involved in crime.

6. Nearby border crossings are very busy and vehicles are subject to minimal checks. Ditto for the ports.

7. Too few officers in your department have the language skills to police the immigrant communities effectively.

8. Senior officers do not assign a high priority to vehicle theft.

Not all of these facilitating conditions can be modified—you cannot change the geographic location of your town—but you should focus on those conditions that are potentially modifiable. For example, your department could assign a higher priority to vehicle theft and could recruit more bilingual officers to allow more effective community policing of immigrant neighborhoods. Or your chief could lobby for more effective vehicle checks at border crossings. Not only should you be identifying the scope for these kinds of actions, but you should be arguing the case for their adoption.

How facilitating conditions make crime ESEER

Like much of the guidance in this manual, the framework for analyzing facilitating conditions is drawn from the field of situational crime prevention, specifically from the five principal techniques of opportunity reduction. These consist of techniques that:

1. Increase the effort needed to commit a particular kind of crime

2. Increase the risks of the crime

3. Reduce the rewards

4. Remove excuses for committing the crime

5. Remove specific temptations or provocations

These opportunity-reducing techniques correspond to five categories of facilitating conditions described in Step 6 those that make crime **E**asy, **S**afe, **E**xcusable, **E**nticing, and **R**ewarding, or **ESEER**. With regard to the list of facilitating conditions for theft of cars for export laid out above, it could be said that: 1–3 make it easy; 7 and 8 make it safe; 5 makes it excusable; 6 makes it tempting; and 4 makes it rewarding. ESEER should make it easier for you to think about and identify the facilitating conditions for any kind of crime.

Police efforts to prevent the repetition of a tragic drowning of illegal immigrants in the U.K.

In February 2004, a group of 23 illegally trafficked Chinese nationals drowned while digging for cockles (a shellfish) in Morecambe Bay, Lancashire. The resulting police investigation took 18 months. It required evidence to be collected in China and from European cockle processing plants, it accumulated 1.5 million pages of documentation (many in Mandarin, Spanish, and French), and it involved many different government agencies in the U.K. and elsewhere. The six-month trial led to manslaughter convictions of three individuals responsible for illegally bringing the Chinese workers to the U.K. and for putting them to work in hazardous conditions.

Despite the enormous cost and effort of prosecuting the case, the Lancashire Constabulary realized that the conditions for a repeat of the tragedy were still in place:

- The scope for vast profits remained. The price of cockles had increased by 400 percent in the four years prior to the tragic drowning.

- Harvesting cockles is simple and relies only on the availability of cheap labor. Chinese networks were still open for recruitment and transportation.

- Illegal immigrants were willing to pay organized criminals up to £20,000 to enter the U.K., this money being deducted weekly from their pitiful wages. Profits were increased by accommodating them in cramped housing and giving them minimal safety equipment.

- Numerous ways to access the vast shoreline provided anonymity to cocklers and their controllers.

- The official permit scheme for harvesting cockles was still lax. On a single day, eight months after the tragedy, 61 Chinese nationals were working illegally on the sands, 48 with fraudulently obtained permits.

- The enforcement of safety regulations had also remained lax. The organized crime group had little interest in the safety of their workers of whom only about 10 percent carried lifejackets, GPS devices, or flares.

- About 100 vehicles transporting as many as 400 cocklers visited the shoreline daily and 80 percent of the vehicles were un-roadworthy, overloaded, or carried roof-riding passengers.

- An estimated 30 percent of cocklers were fraudulently claiming welfare benefits, at an estimated cost per year of £1,200,000.

- U.K. Border controls remained open to exploitation, and the risk of deportation was low. Immigration authorities had insufficient resources to detain potential illegal immigrants, who were released and asked to report to the immigration office at a later date.

Fearing a repeat of the tragedy, the Lancashire Constabulary decided to modify as many of these facilitating conditions as possible. An important priority was to reduce the anonymity of the organized crime group and the exploited workers. The permit scheme was strengthened, but the real innovation was to use existing legitimate workers to assist in identifying illegal workers. This was accomplished through the provision of a "muster point" (a catering van) in a safe location on the sands to communicate legal, procedural, and safety issues. A notice board displayed vehicle and contact details of workers on the sands, tide times, cockle bed information, as well as agency details.

This brought various benefits. Twelve hundred regulated workers were recorded in the new permit scheme and fraudulent unemployment benefit claims were reduced by 20 percent in the first year. Un-roadworthy vehicle usage reduced by 84 percent, with roof-riding eradicated. All workers started to carry personal life-saving equipment. Sea rescue deployments to save cocklers dropped from 34 in 2004 to 1 in 2005. The workforce went on to form their own shellfish association which met weekly and performed a self-policing function.

Detectives uncovered new information about migrant trafficking between China and the U.K., including who were the criminals and associates, how the profits were made, and how money was laundered. This information was insufficient to prosecute offenders, but shining a spotlight on them meant that they were operating in a more hostile environment with associates becoming worried that police attention might be drawn to their businesses. This helps explain why the criminals involved could not simply displace their illegal cockling activities elsewhere in England.

READ MORE:
Stuart Kirby. 2010. "Policing Mobile Criminality: Towards a Situational Crime Prevention Approach to Organised Crime." In *Situational Prevention of Organised Crimes*, ed. Karen Bullock, Ronald V. Clarke, and Nick Tilley. Cullompton, Devon: Willan Publishing.

CRIMINOLOGISTS HAVE BEEN PREOCCUPIED BY THE QUESTION OF CRIMINAL MOTIVATION—why is that certain people, or kinds of people, become involved in crime and delinquency? In trying to answer this question, they have used hundreds of studies to probe into the backgrounds of offenders and have identified a vast range of possible contributory factors of upbringing, biology, personality, and social circumstances.

These theories are of limited practical value in your work as a crime analyst. This is because police can do nothing to alter an offender's history and little to change society. In any case, at a more down to earth level, motives for crime generally derive from common human failings such as greed, anger, covetousness, and the wish for such things as excitement, revenge, respect, and sexual release. Although some understanding of these commonplace motives may be helpful in analyzing particular categories of crime, knowing *why* crimes are committed is usually less useful than knowing *how* they are committed. This is because a detailed understanding of the *modus operandi* for a specific category of crime reveals many points for opportunity-reducing interventions. This is evident from Table 5, adapted from an analysis by Derek Cornish, formerly of the London School of Economics, showing steps in stealing a car from a parking lot and associated interventions.

Apart from showing a range of possible interventions, the table reveals a little appreciated fact: even a crime as simple as taking a car from a parking lot is not over in a flash, as we tend to think. In fact, it can take quite long to plan, prepare for, and execute—and this table does not even show what happens after the car is taken, how it might be used, sold, or concealed.

If we assume the car has been stolen to order for export, we would need to include, as a preliminary; receiving the instructions about which kind of car to steal, where best to find such a car, and where to deliver it. After the car has been removed from the lot, we would need information about the subsequent stages in getting the car to the ultimate buyer in another country. These include:

1. Bringing the car to a secure location where its identity may be changed and it might be disassembled

2. Storing it until ready to transport across border

3. Loading it in a sealed container onto a ship, either whole or disassembled

4. Or simply driving it across the border

5. At the destination handing it over to a local contact

Table 5. Stealing a car from a parking lot and possible interventions

STEPS	POSSIBLE INTERVENTIONS
Hook-up with co-offender	Use informants in convergent settings (see Step 12)
Get tools (screwdriver, slide-hammer, duplicate keys)	Control sales of duplicate keys and slide-hammers
Enter parking lot	Parking lot barriers; attendants; few entrances
Loiter unobtrusively	Cameras and/or regular patrols to deter loiterers
Reject alarmed cars Choose suitable vehicle	Visible protection of tempting vehicles
Enter car (duplicate keys, use screwdriver)	Cameras to monitor suspicious behavior; improve natural surveillance of lot
Break ignition lock (slide-hammer) or hot-wire ignition	Vehicle alarm to alert security; vehicle immobilizer
Exit parking lot in car	Attendants or other exit barriers; Vehicle-tracking system activated

Source: Cornish 1994.

6.   Or having it collected at the dock by such person

7.   If necessary having it reassembled

8.   Legally registering it if necessary

9.   Selling it on the open market or to private buyer

A detailed understanding of these stages would reveal many other possible interventions, though you might be interested primarily in the first four of them because they occur locally and you might therefore be in a better position to impede them, than stages 5–9 that take place overseas.

Laying out the sequence of stages for a problematic gathering can also reveal many intervention points. This is illustrated in Table 6, taken from a POP Guide on dealing with five sequential stages of student party riots: Initial planning; Preassembly preparation;

Assembly; Assembled gathering; and Dispersal. The several steps falling under each of these stages yield many possible points of intervention.

READ MORE:

Derek Cornish. 1994. "The Procedural Analysis of Offending and its Relevance for Situational Prevention." Vol. 3 of *Crime Prevention Studies*, 151–196. Monsey, New York: Criminal Justice Press.

Table 6. Intervening to prevent a student party riot

	INTERVENTION	HOW IT WORKS
Stage 1: Initial planning		
1	Create a multiagency task force	Assembles community resources, and clarifies the roles and responsibilities of the groups involved
2	Require students to obtain a permit	Gives advance notice of a gathering, sets standards for the event, and holds hosts responsible for meeting the standards
3	Assign police to assist the hosts	Officers help students to meet legal requirements for a gathering
4	Increase penalties for rioting	Deters students from destructive behavior at the gathering
5	Partner with the media to influence student and community perceptions	Increases positive perceptions of the event and perceptions of risk for those interested in causing a disturbance
6	Work with landlords to ensure renter compliance	Creates more risk for hosting disruptive gatherings on rented property; encourages landlords to assist in preventing these
7	Control alcohol distribution	Reduces student alcohol consumption, underage drinking and purchasing of alcohol, and drunken driving
8	Provide alternative entertainment	Reduces the number of people at a single gathering; provides alternative recreation in a more controlled setting
Stage 2: Preassembly preparation		
9	Ask students to form "student patrols"	Reduces the need for official interventions
10	"Sanitize" the gathering location	Removes objects that can become a safety hazard
11	Monitor ads for gatherings	Notifies authorities of large gatherings in advance
12	Limit parking	Increases the effort needed to attend; removes targets that may be vandalized; clears exits in case of an emergency
13	Close or control traffic flow	Reduces pedestrian injuries; prevents students from bringing in large, dangerous objects

INTERVENTION	HOW IT WORKS
Stage 3: Assembling	
14 Provide transportation to the event	Facilitates orderly arrival; reduces the number of cars; prevents attendees from bringing large quantities of alcohol
15 Establish a positive police presence	Reduces anonymity and facilitates communication
16 Establish and control perimeters	Prevents the gathering from spreading into the surrounding areas
Stage 4: Assembled gathering	
17 Use alternative deployment methods	Gives officers a tactical advantage over car patrols
18 Use visual deterrents to misconduct	Reminds those attending of the consequences of rioting
19 Videotape the assembled gathering	Reduces anonymity; assists in subsequent investigations
20 Site the media around the gathering	Breaks-up the cohesion of large groups
21 Watch for flashpoints	Immediate intervention can prevent a violent outbreak
22 Standardize the procedure to deal with disturbances	Helps stop violence as soon as it begins
Stage 5: Dispersal	
23 Provide transport from the event	Controls dispersal; reduces drunken driving
24 Facilitate orderly dispersal	Breaks up the gathering before a disturbance begins

Source: Tamara Madensen and John E. Eck. 2006. *Student Party Riots*. Problem Specific Guides No 40. Washington, D.C.: U.S. Department of Justice, Office of Community Oriented Policing Services.

IN STEPS 8 AND 9 WE NOTED THAT MOST OFFENDER GROUPS ARE LOOSE KNIT AFFILIATIONS OF INDIVIDUALS, rather than tightly controlled hierarchical organizations. How do these groups form, how do they persist, and how do new loose knit groups reform when other groups are broken up?

Convergent settings play an important role in these processes. Marcus Felson describes an offender convergent setting as a stable and predictable place where offenders, or potential offenders, can meet and form alliances. A place may be a convergent setting only at particular times. For example, a nightclub may offer a variety of performances throughout the week, but on Friday nights, the management caters to a particular crowd by providing music they find appealing. Potential offenders in this crowd know that if they show up on Friday nights they will find others with the same criminal interests.

The parking lot of a street corner convenience store may provide another example of a convergent setting. The store serves as an anchor for offenders by providing food and shelter for those hanging out. It also provides a ready excuse to be at the location, should a police officer stop the offender.

Convergent settings serve offenders in five ways:

1. **They bring together offenders and potential offenders who would not meet otherwise.** So they provide a spawning ground for offender groups. Many legitimate settings do this. High schools, for example, bring juveniles together who would not meet in other circumstances. The vast majority of these youth do not get into serious trouble, but a few students band together to commit crimes. Any youth gathering spot can serve as a convergent setting that can create groups that would not form in the absence of the convergent setting. Entertainment zones also serve such functions. A few mosques have served as convergent settings that allow Islamic extremists to meet and recruit potential new terrorists. Institutions for offenders—such as drug rehabilitation centers, half-way houses, and prisons—can become convergent settings.

2. **They provide a venue for strangers to observe each other and build sufficient trust and knowledge that they can work together.** If the setting only brings people together for very short intervals, then group formation is difficult. The ability to hang out and talk without looking suspicious is important.

3. **They provide convenient ways for offenders who already know each other to meet.** If an offender knows a bar to be a place where other offenders are likely to be present on a Saturday night, then he just needs to show up. He does not have to make specific plans with other offenders.

4. **They help groups replace members.** Without a replacement process, groups disappear. This is very common. With a convergent setting, it is easy for groups to recruit new members. When group members know that others at the setting are potential offenders this allows easy recruiting. Offenders who want to join a group know that if they routinely show up at a convergent setting, they have a good chance of becoming a member of a group.

5. **In private places they allow group members to meet without scrutiny.** Such places supply venues for initiation rituals, planning of complex offenses, and social support. Whereas public convergent settings are usually created for legitimate reasons and exploited for illegitimate reasons, private offender convergent settings are usually created to serve illegitimate ends.

Figure 7. Convergent settings are sometimes crime hot spots

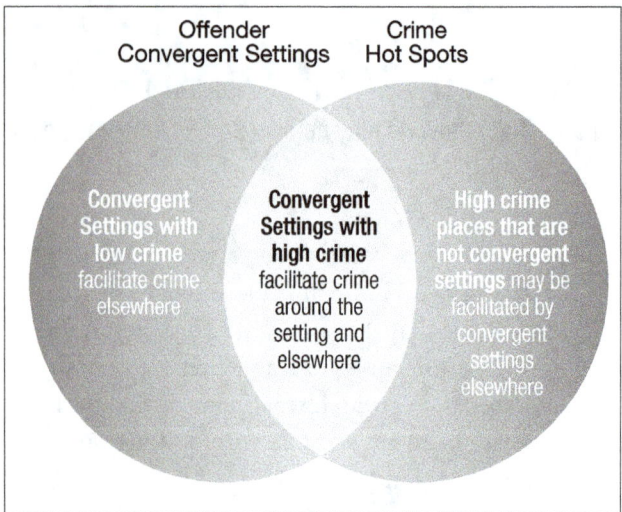

Convergent settings may also be crime hot spots (see Figure 7). A bar that is a convergent setting for offenders attracts offenders who might take advantage of targets in the area. The opposite is also true. An active drug dealing location may become a convergent setting because it attracts people who want to become part of the drug trade. These wannabe members can provide a temporary labor pool—for carrying messages, serving as look outs, steering customers, or holding guns, drugs, or money—and while doing this can be evaluated for recruitment as permanent members of the group.

Analysts can detect convergent settings that are also crime hot spots through crime mapping. Convergent settings that are not crime hot spots will require you to find other methods of detection. Informants, offender surveillance and tracking, and other techniques will be more helpful than crime maps.

Convergent settings are not always physical places. For example, terrorists can use Internet websites as **virtual** convergent settings. Such websites allow people from around the world to meet and exchange information. Child pornography can be distributed through virtual convergent settings that accelerate the formation of pornography rings.

What should you do about offender convergent settings?

The most important thing is to look for them and exploit them for purposes of collecting data about offenders. Convergent settings can be a rich source of intelligence data describing active offenders: how they are organized, and what they may be doing.

Changing the setting so it does not facilitate offender groups is another important option. This is particularly true if the convergent setting is also a crime hot spot. Since many such settings are public places used by non-offenders, you should give preference to finding ways the place can continue to function without aiding offenders. This is possible if the owners of the place are not involved in crime. If the owner is aligned with the offender group, then regulatory or civil court action may be required to seize control of the place and keep it from being used by offenders.

There can be a conflict between using the offender convergent setting as a source of intelligence data and disrupting offender convergence. Allowing an offender convergent setting to operate in order to gain intelligence data also allows the offender group to continue committing crimes. This may be worthwhile if either a) many non-offenders legitimately use the setting, b) if closing the place simply displaces the convergent setting, or c) the offender group disrupted by the setting's closure is highly likely to be replaced by some other offender group.

On the other hand, altering a convergent setting to reduce crime may cut off vital intelligence and make it difficult to keep track of offender groups. If closing the setting reduces crime, and limits offender groups from reestablishing, then the loss of intelligence is probably a reasonable cost. This seems likely when the convergent setting is the locus of a crime hot spot.

Consequently, before making a decision about how to address a convergent setting, police should consider who else, besides offenders, uses the place; the availability of alternative convergent settings that offenders can displace to; and the chances that another offender group will exploit the situation.

READ MORE:

Marcus Felson. 2003. "The Process of Co-Offending." In *Theory for Practice in Situational Crime Prevention*, ed., Martha Smith and Derek B. Cornish. Vol. 16 of *Crime Prevention Studies*. Monsey, New York: Criminal Justice Press.

POLICE WILL OFTEN TRY TO REMOVE KEY MEMBERS OF A CRIMINAL GROUP on the grounds that the broken up group will no longer be a problem. If its members are not replaced, or replacement takes a very long time, then disruption can work.

Before looking at the different forms of replacement, let us examine a generic recruitment process used to varying extent by most offender groups that can replace their members:

- The group must make contact with a potential new member. Convergent settings are useful at this stage and networks of offenders can refer potential recruits to group members.

- Screening or conducting the equivalent of a background check must be undertaken. This may be limited—such as checking on the potential recruit's reputation—or it might be extensive—for example, designed to weed out police operatives or informants.

- Screening may be coupled with testing or testing may be done separately. Testing might involve carrying out simple tasks to see how the subject performs, initiation rites, or even training. Screening and testing will depend on the risks associated with recruiting the wrong person, and on the skill level needed to carry out the tasks.

- Finally, the recruit might be employed as a peripheral member to carry out some minor tasks. Depending on the size and nature of the group, the subject may be promoted.

These stages assume varying importance for different forms of replacement.

Forms of group replacement

There are four forms of replacement (as illustrated in Figure 8) that you need to be concerned with:

1. **Full group replacement.** This occurs if the targeted group is incapacitated and totally replaced by another group. Many offender groups have limited ability to replace members, or even desire to do so. A group of young men on a street corner may have formed because they grew up near each other and have known each other for a long time. The members trust each other. Arresting and incarcerating most of them may disband the group, but the remaining members may have little interest in recruiting new members. However, another group of similarly situated young men may then move into the criminal niche that the first group has vacated. While this may not occur immediately, it is likely to occur if the conditions that fostered the first group are still present. Full replacement may also come after groups fight it out for who will take the territory or businesses of the disrupted group.

2. **Fracturing a group.** Removing members of a group may incapacitate the targeted group, but the remaining members may start up several smaller groups and continue the criminal behavior of the now defunct first group. The cottage industry theory of midlevel drug dealing suggests that this is common. According to this theory, many midlevel trafficking groups are loose knit marriages of convenience that form and reform. It could be that fracturing such a group facilitates recruitment of new crime participants because those offenders left on the street might seek out new partners. Fracturing can generate new groups if the conditions that facilitate group crime persist; the remaining members continue to take advantage of these conditions.

3. **Replacement of peripheral members.** If the group is made up of a core set of members surrounded by peripheral participants, then replacement of these peripheral members is possible when police remove peripheral members. The shell of disposable members, who undertake the riskiest activities, protects the core. This is common in retail drug trafficking—core distributors hire locals to sell the drugs and take the risk. It is also used in fraud groups,

Figure 8. Forms of group replacement

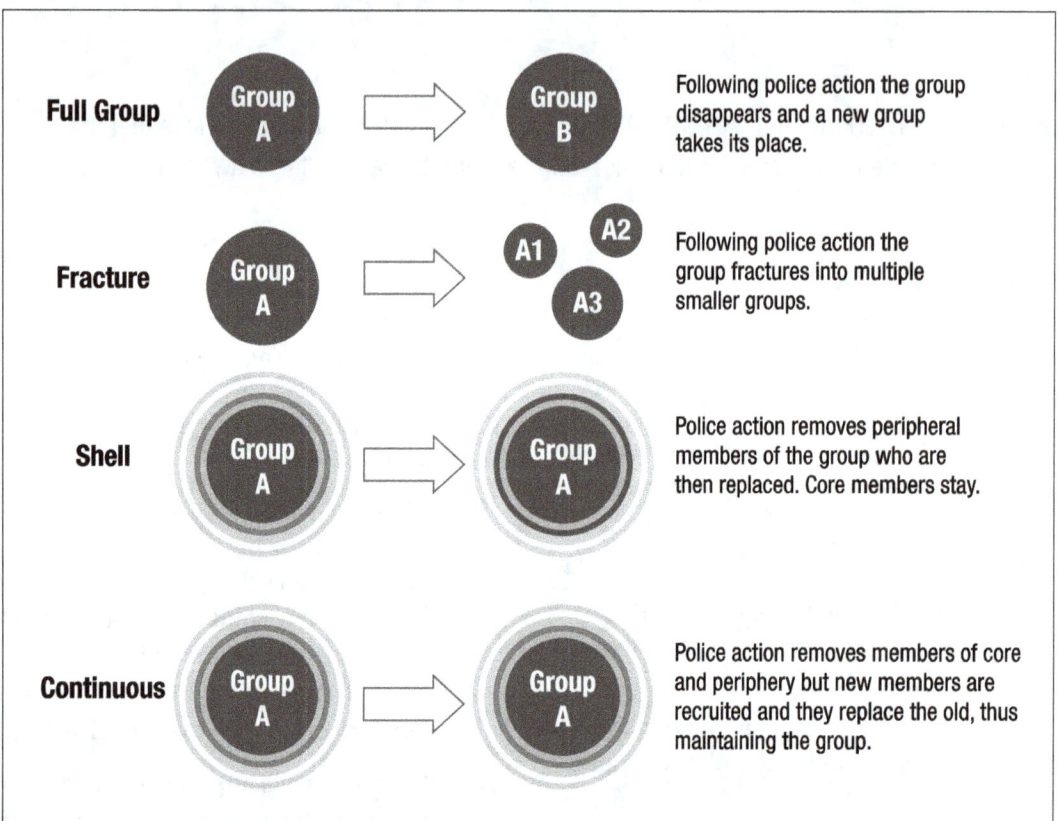

where the core players use disposable agents (who might not know the core members' names) to do the dirty work. In these circumstances, unlike continuous replacement, there is no expectation that members in the shell will ever advance to the core.

4. **Continuous replacement.** Some groups have recruitment practices that allow them to bring in new members and promote them. Enforcement may remove members from the core and periphery but the recruitment and promotion processes allow the group to continue its criminal activities. Continuous replacement requires the criminal group to have sufficient size that it can continuously suffer losses and maintain its basic structure. Any criminal group that is large and has existed for many years while under law enforcement pressure has probably mastered this strategy. Outlaw motorcycle gangs may be a good example of this: some have existed for decades with turnover at all levels of the organization.

Conditions for recruitment and replacement

The environmental opportunity structure within which the group operates creates two conditions necessary for recruitment and replacement:

1. The group cannot persist if the environment does not facilitate the particular criminal behavior the group carries out. The environment must provide a set of conditions—the opportunity structure— that permits the group to function. The group is adapted to this opportunity structure. Radical changes in the opportunity structure will limit all four forms of replacement discussed above.

2. There must also be an opportunity structure for recruitment and replacement. One example is convergent settings that we discussed in Step 12. Convergent settings allow offenders to meet other potential partners and permit group members to routinely meet potential new members.

Intelligence analysis needs to focus on the group's environment to understand these two conditions.

Replacement of peripheral members

A police official we interviewed described the following example of the use of shell replacement. In the 2000s, police agencies in eastern Massachusetts took dozens of reports from victims of the "Big Carrot" scam. Victims were called at work by someone claiming to be "Jim, your UPS driver." "Jim" divulged that his brother worked at Sears, Best Buy, or a similar "big box" store that was overstocked on big-screen TVs, or other high-end electronics, and the victims could get a great deal if they would pay cash. The victims met "Jim's brother" outside the store, turned over the cash, and got a handwritten receipt and instructions to pick up their merchandise at the loading dock. By the time they discovered there was no merchandise, Jim's brother had fled.

While many departments arrested dozens of men, they were unable to crack the core group who made the initial calls. They were never the ones to meet victims, collect the money, and hand over the "receipts." Instead, they hired ex-cons to serve as the "runners," who were the ones arrested. None of them knew the names of their bosses, and they were simply replaced with new stooges for the next round of scams. Although police did develop some intelligence on the ringleaders, as of 2010, police still occasionally received reports of these crimes, with no change in *modus operandi*.

14

INTERVIEWING OFFENDERS CAN GIVE YOU USEFUL INFORMATION ABOUT WHY THEY COMMIT THEIR CRIMES, how they decide to commit them, and how they carry them out. You do not need to interview a "representative" or even a large sample to gain considerable insight into the group you are examining. You can sometimes conduct the interviews with offenders who are temporarily in custody, awaiting a court appearance. You might be able to get officers handling the case to ask the questions on your behalf, but you will have to brief them very carefully about the information you want and why. Even after release from jail or prison, you may find it useful to see if offenders are willing to talk about how they and others committed crimes.

Cooperation depends critically on the content of the questions. Make it clear that you are not looking for information about specific crimes they have committed or information about specific co-offenders. Treat the offender as an expert whose insights you are seeking. If you make clear that you are interested in generalities about the crimes in question—how targets are selected, how crimes are committed, ways of recruiting members, etc.—you can get much useful information. Offenders are often willing to talk openly about their crimes if they see no risks for themselves in doing so. This has been shown in many research studies, with different kinds of offenders. If you have little experience with such interviews, seek out an investigator with a reputation for putting offenders at ease and gaining useful information.

It is sometimes important to obtain information from a larger, more representative group. You might also feel it is important to interview active offenders who have not been caught. In such cases, your department may need to contract with a private research firm to conduct the interviews or with a university researcher. Such interviews are commonly undertaken by researchers studying a particular problem (see both Boxes for examples).

Where there is no need to talk with active offenders, they can be interviewed in prison. Again, if you use outside researchers to conduct such interviews, you must brief them carefully about what you need to know. Your agency will have to work out confidentiality and nondisclosure agreements with the researcher so they do not have to report which offenders said what.

Interviewing procedures

Professor Scott Decker of Arizona State University, who has conducted many interviews with offenders, breaks up the task into the eight steps discussed below:

1. *Establish the goal of the interviews before you start.* What gap would the interviews fill and how will that help in your analytic efforts? Do you need to understand the offender's motives, co-offending strategies, and target selection techniques? How will you use this information? It is important to devise a questionnaire to guide your interview.

2. *Decide who to interview.* Interviewing just any member of the group might not be worthwhile. High-rate offenders would usually be more knowledgeable about the operations of the group, other members' involvement, group objectives, and organizational structure. Seeking out the right person for the interview is therefore important.

3. *Determine who should conduct the interview.* This is mostly a matter of who has the skill and the access to the offenders. As mentioned above, if the offender is in police custody, a skilled officer might be able to interview the offender if you provide the questions that need answering. If you have the interviewing skills then you can do it. Interviewing active offenders who have not been caught poses greater difficulties. Locating them and interviewing them 'on their own turf' will require advance intelligence about where these groups operate. In most cases, someone from the police could conduct the interviews, again, with your guidance, but it might be possible to enlist the help of skilled researchers in this task.

4. *Convince offenders to participate.* This is sometimes difficult, although research suggests that many convicted offenders are willing to talk about their own feats. You should consult your local legal counsel to find out what inducements can legally be offered to these offenders in return for their participation, which do not violate policies and professional ethics.

5. *Record the answers.* Use of a tape recorder will allow the information to be transcribed and analyzed in detail. On the other hand, using a tape recorder may jeopardize cooperation.

6. *Analyze interview results.* This can be helped by using hypertext analysis software packages, such as Folio Views or Ask Sam, which allow you to quickly sort through the interview results and identify patterns.

7. *Sort out the truth.* This can be done by repeated questioning to look for consistency, interviewing different offenders about the same issue, or comparing what they say to what is already known through other sources. If you already have some knowledge about the group whose member you are interviewing, that knowledge will help sort truth from fiction.

8. *Use the interview results in problem solving.* Successful interviews will dictate response strategies that you can suggest to your police department. The Boston Operation Ceasefire, for example, used interviews with active gang members to learn about their preferences for guns and the gang's dependence on drug dealing. The results from these interviews led to the use of directed patrol against gang drug sales whenever there were shootings.

Theft of supplies and medicines in hospitals: What nurses said…

Dean Dabney interviewed 25 registered nurses in three hospitals to find out more about the theft of supplies and medicines. Almost all the nurses said that they took supplies from hospital stock, and claimed that this was accepted behavior among nurses who generally believed it was 'kind of compensation.' Thefts of over-the-counter drugs, including painkillers, were very common and were never reported to the hospital authorities. Thefts of non-narcotic prescription medicine was also common; in these cases, nurses take advantage of the lag between the pharmacists realizing that the patient is no longer taking the medicines and when they quit sending them. Thefts of narcotic medicines by nurses, although rare, also occur, but are much more likely to be reported by other nurses.

Source: Dean Dabney. 2000. Neutralization and deviance in the workplace: Theft of supplies and medicines by hospital nurses. In *Deviance and Deviants,* ed. Richard Tewksbury and Patricia Gagne. Los Angeles: Roxbury Publishing.

Incorporating offender interviews in problem solving

The Cincinnati Police Department and researchers at the University of Cincinnati worked together to use offender and victim interviews to reduce street robberies. Police were interested in whether groups of offenders were involved, if the robbers targeted Hispanic victims, and several other questions. Police and researchers developed a set of questions. Two detectives interviewed robbery arrestees and victims, and taped the interviews. At the university, the tapes were transcribed, the transcriptions coded so they could be analyzed, and then the coded date was analyzed. The results showed that the offenders were probably not operating in stable groups, but they had a distinct preference for Hispanic victims who robbers rightfully believed were unlikely to report the robberies. Police used these results to inform members of the Hispanic community in the area.

READ MORE:

Scott Decker. 2005. *Using Offender Interviews to Inform Police Problem Solving.* Problem-Oriented Guides for Police. Problem-Solving Tools Series, No. 3. Washington, D.C.: U.S. Department of Justice, Office of Community Oriented Policing Services.

15 TAP THE KNOWLEDGE OF OFFICERS

PATROL OFFICERS AND INVESTIGATORS ARE IMPORTANT SOURCES OF INTELLIGENCE DATA and tapping their knowledge can be extremely helpful to you. This point is often addressed by developing better procedures for information sharing. Data sharing procedures can help, but they do not go far enough. This is because information sharing can only help when two conditions are met: someone has data of potential use for intelligence, and someone knows that the data is potentially valuable. Former U.S. Secretary of Defense, Donald Rumsfeld, has developed a classification based on these conditions, which we apply in the four cells of Table 7.

If the data is known to be of value to address an offender group, and an officer has the information, then the emphasis should be placed on data sharing (cell 1). However, when police have the data, but do not know its value, then intelligence analysts need to spend more time briefing patrol officers and investigators about what sorts of data is useful. This is sharing information about targets (cell 2).

When no one in the police department has the data, then information or target sharing will not help. If intelligence analysts can identify specific gaps in their knowledge (they know the value of the data, but do not have it), then focused efforts to gain the data can be designed and launched (cell 3).

The most difficult circumstance is that no one knows that the data is of value (though it is), and no one in the police department has the data (cell 4). There is no satisfactory solution to this problem, but there are three practices that can help:

1. If patrol officers or investigators have diverse experiences with a group of offenders, bringing them together to exchange ideas and experiences may be useful. Discussions among police who have very different experiences with the group may challenge some basic assumptions about the group and reveal potential knowledge gaps. The purpose of the discussion is to explore disagreements; consensus and agreement is not the goal.

Table 7. Four problems with using the knowledge of police officers

FOUR PROBLEMS WITH USING THE KNOWLEDGE OF POLICE OFFICERS		
	Data's value is known	Data's value is unknown
Data is known to police	Cell 1 Someone within the police agency has the data, and they know it is useful for intelligence. Improvement in information sharing may help.	Cell 2 Someone within the police agency has the data, but the value of this data is unknown. Sharing target information may help.
Data is unknown to police	Cell 3 No one in the police agency has the data, but it is known that if the data were available, it would be valuable. Targeted data collection may be helpful.	Cell 4 No one in the police agency has the data, and even if that data was collected its value would not be known. Discussions among police familiar with the problem, surveys of police personnel, or theory driven data collection may help.

2. Data may be dispersed among many individuals so that no individual understands that they have useful data. Surveys of officers and investigators can identify: (a) patterns of knowledge that no one was aware of; (b) hidden differences in police understanding; and (c) knowledge gaps that can be targeted for additional data collection. In the late 1990s, the Washington/Baltimore High Intensity Drug Trafficking Area (W/B HIDTA) conducted an annual survey of its many squads to assess commonalities and differences among the offender groups being investigated. The surveys suggested that for the most part, the groups being addressed by the investigative squads were small to moderate in size, not hierarchically organized, and not long lived. This was useful strategic intelligence for the W/B HIDTA.

3. Training officers, investigators, and intelligence analysts in environmental criminology theories may help them understand the problem being addressed. Discussing ways to address offender groups (based on research and experience) can also reduce the circumstances under which police do not know the data they need to collect.

Barriers to information sharing

Patrol officers and investigators may sometimes be unwilling to share information for reasons discussed below. Here we use the familiar framework of risks, effort, rewards, excuses, and provocations.

Risks of Sharing. If officers feel there is greater risk for sharing information than not sharing, then little sharing will take place. Have clear policies and procedures for sharing and hold people accountable for sharing, when sharing is legally permitted. Hold supervisors accountable for assuring adequate sharing.

Effort of sharing. If information sharing is easy, more information will be shared. Reducing the effort necessary to pass information along can be facilitated by making it convenient. If two units routinely need to share information, this will happen more readily when they are located in close physical proximity. Reducing the paperwork burden can also reduce the effort, though this may interfere with holding supervisors accountable for sharing.

Rewards for not sharing. If officers or their units get more rewards for holding on to data than for sharing it, they will not share. Look for ways of crediting officers for sharing. If officers do not learn how the data they provided helped, then they are less likely to share in the future. Giving feedback on the utility of the data increases rewards for sharing. Further, if officers are only asked to give data, but seldom receive data, then they will have less incentive to share. Look for opportunities to provide them with useful data.

Excuses for not sharing. There are four common excuses officers use to avoid sharing intelligence data: it is not my job; there is no one to tell; others already know this; and, I did not know it was useful. Policies and procedures, training, and supervision can address the first excuse. Ensuring that intelligence analysts are known to officers can address the second. Holding discussions with officers and investigators about targets can address the last two excuses.

Provocations for not sharing. If officers and investigators have bad relationships with intelligence analysts, then they are more likely to withhold data than if they have good relationships. While policies, procedures, training, and supervision are necessary, they are not sufficient to assure information sharing. Good personal relationships are essential.

DISASTER PREPARATION ALREADY REQUIRES YOUR DEPARTMENT TO WORK CLOSELY WITH THE MAYOR OR CITY manager, as well as with other city agencies such as fire, emergency medical, hospitals, and schools. Make use of this partnership when gathering intelligence about criminal groups that you may be investigating. In addition, forming partnerships with private security and businesses in your city can help your department in gathering intelligence about criminal groups. This is especially important for dealing with suspected terrorist groups.

Businesses are an important source of information about the activities of criminal groups. For example, banks, check-cashing establishments, and money-transfer stations, such as Western Union, can tell you about suspicious financial transactions or financial transactions of suspect groups; car rental agencies, motels, and real estate agents can give you information about newcomers and transients; and private security practitioners can inform you about organized fraud that might be funding terrorism. Your department should take charge of the partnership, but to obtain full cooperation it should give private sector colleagues public credit for their contributions.

In the United States, private security employees outnumber the police by three to one. They are responsible for the security of most of your jurisdiction's infrastructure and provide visible crime control in the places where people spend much of their daily lives: at work, on public transport, in educational facilities, in shopping malls, and even in gated communities. One of the best ways to approach the larger businesses in your community is through their corporate security officers, but there are many other security professionals in your community who could provide you with valuable help. These include local security consultants, the suppliers of guard services, and installers of security hardware and systems.

You might think you already have good informal contacts with this group, facilitated by the many retired police officers employed within their ranks. However, the Department of Homeland Security recommends that, to serve the goal of preventing terrorism, police chiefs in larger jurisdictions should consider formalizing relationships with private security through coordination agreements or memorandums of understanding. Formalization shows employees from both sides that the partnership

is an organizational priority. Specifically, it will help your department do the following:

- Safeguard the critical infrastructure in your community that is protected by private security and ensure rapid recovery in the event of an attack

- Obtain effective help from private security in emergencies

- Improve the flow of information—in both directions. Partnering will allow you to communicate threat information to the private sector efficiently and, conversely, it will allow the private sector direct access to the right people when they need help or want to report information.

- Make use of private-sector knowledge on topics that your department might know little about, such as organized fraud or cybercrime

- Obtain access to private-sector resources and facilities that will help you meet training and operational needs

Perhaps the most critical issue concerns the handling of sensitive information. Your department may be uncomfortable sharing information—especially about terrorist groups—with companies owned by foreign entities and it may not be legally permitted to share information that private security requests, such as criminal histories. For their part, private security may fear that proprietary business information could become public as a result of Freedom of Information Act requests. They might avoid speaking candidly at partnership meetings because competitors could learn about their problems, or because they might be charged with antitrust violations if they discuss inappropriate topics. Finally, they might not report instances of cybercrime because your department might then seize their records and computers. In a word, this all boils down to mutual trust which takes time and patient negotiation to develop.

Getting started

- Clarify the purpose of the partnership and set goals for improved collaboration and coordination

- Spell out what the partnership must do to accomplish its mission

- Identify the resources the partnership will need to meet its goals and find ways to secure these materials

- Find a physical and logistical home for the partnership and appoint a police officer to coordinate its activities

- Decide how the partnership members will communicate, both routinely and in emergencies

- Create an identity for the partnership through the use of a logo, brochure, or website, and use this identity to obtain funds and recruit members

READ MORE:

John Dempsey. 2008. *Introduction to Private Security.* Thomson Higher Education.

Graeme Newman and Ronald Clarke. 2008. *Policing Terrorism: An Executive's Guide.* Washington, D.C.: U.S. Department of Justice, Office of Community Oriented Policing Services.

The Law Enforcement-Private Security Consortium. 2009. *Operation Partnership: Trends and Practices in Law Enforcement and Private Security Collaboration.* Washington, D.C.: U.S. Department of Justice, Office of Community Oriented Policing Services. www.cops.usdoj. gov/Publications/e08094224-OpPartnership.pdf.

YOU CANNOT OVERESTIMATE THE IMPORTANCE OF THE COMMUNITY: it is the source of most police knowledge about offender groups. Offender groups will attempt to control what community members know about them and what they pass on to police. So, if there is friction between community members and the police, offender groups will exploit this weakness.

By community, we mean people who live, work, study, or play in the area. There are four main ways that the community can assist police in addressing offender groups, corresponding to the four stages of SARA (Step 5).

Identifying concerns and problems (scanning)

Community members are the first to encounter offender groups, if not as victims then as neighbors, acquaintances, customers, or tenants. Before police are aware of a new offender group, people in the community have often detected its presence. This may be one of the greatest values of community policing— taking community concerns seriously and allowing the police to learn early about developing problems.

While police should pay close attention to the community, you should not take all views expressed by the public as equally valid. You should treat expressions of concern regarding offender groups as hypotheses that you need to test (Step 21). Table 8 illustrates this point. Community members may express no concern about some group behaviors—because they do not find these troublesome; they are intimidated; they gain from the behaviors; or they are unaware of them. Police enquiries may indicate that this lack of concern is valid (cell 1) or that there is a serious problem but the public is not expressing concern (cell 2). In contrast, the community may find some group behaviors very troublesome. Analysis may indicate that these concerns are misdirected (cell 3) or that they are fundamentally sound (cell 4). Distinguishing between cells 3 and 4 is often difficult. Community members may have important insights that go beyond data available to the police, but they can also misperceive situations and demand actions that are inappropriate, costly, or violate civil liberties.

Table 8. Community concerns and community problems

	NO EVIDENCE OF A PROBLEM	EVIDENCE OF A PROBLEM
No expressed community concern	1. Issues that can be ignored. But you cannot rule out the possibility of a deeply hidden problem.	2. Determine why the community is unconcerned with the problem and consider expanding work with the community to address the problem.
Expressed community concern	3. Seek data to determine if the concern is valid, or if evidence is negative, determine why some members of the public believe there is a problem. The public's concerns may need redefining. This may not be an issue intelligence analysis can address.	4. Some community members may be in a good position to assist with gathering intelligence.

Knowledge about offender groups (analysis)

The most obvious way community members can help is by providing data on the offender group. You can expect four groups of people to have useful knowledge of the group:

1. **Co-offenders** are community members who are members of the group or knowingly assist the group in its activities.

2. **Victims** are people directly harmed by the group's criminal behaviors. (Many of these victims, especially of group violence, may be co-offenders.)

3. **Place managers** are the owners and managers of businesses, residences, and other facilities that the group uses. These managers may be unaware of the group's activities, they may know what is going on but choose to ignore it, or they may knowingly work with the group.

4. **Others** include neighbors, businesses, delivery workers, and government workers who frequent the area and encounter the group.

The value of the information will depend on how well these people know the group, their physical proximity to the group's area of operation, and the degree to which the group's behavior influences their lives. If the group is well integrated into the community, this might limit the information you can expect to get from the public

Possible ways to address group (response)

Just as community members vary in their knowledge of a group, so does their ability to assist in dealing with the group. Those most knowledgeable may not be those who can do the most about the group. Those who can provide the greatest assistance in addressing problems may not be those who know most about the group. Residents of an apartment building, for example, may know a lot about a gang that uses the building, but they may not be able to do much about it. On the other hand, the owner of the building, who may know the least about the group, has the power to change lease conditions and alter the building's physical environment.

There are three ways members of the public can assist:

1. They have resources and legal powers that can be used against the group. Place managers provide a good example, particularly if the group relies on specific locations for their activities.

2. They have expertise that can be applied to the solution. Such expertise can vary from the ability to help remove an abandoned building or clean up a vacant lot used by a gang, to having computer training sufficient to create a database and website for a community group.

3. They create community and political support for actions against the group. This can be particularly important if the offender group is networked with elected officials, or there is a need to put pressure on business or property owners who facilitate the group's activities. At minimum, you do not want substantial community antagonism to the police efforts, so winning and maintaining public support can be important for solving crime problems. Selling a solution to a community after it has been decided on behind closed doors is often more difficult than including community members in problem solving from the beginning—even if this raises concerns about how much intelligence information can be shared with participating community members.

Perceptions of effectiveness (assessment)

The final way community members can assist intelligence analysis is the evaluation of police actions. If public perceptions are important, then poll community members after police actions to determine if they perceive a reduction in the problem. This can be as simple as informal discussions with members of the public or as rigorous as randomly sampling the public and interviewing them about how they view the problem. For example, if the police take action against an offender group shaking down business owners for protection money, it would be useful to have covert conversations with business owners to determine if they are still receiving threats.

Even if such data is not used to evaluate effectiveness, sharing evaluation results with the community is useful. It may be that while there is strong quantitative evidence of a reduction in the group crime problem, members of the public can point to exceptions that you need to address.

GEOGRAPHIC INFORMATION SYSTEMS (GIS) CAN ASSIST THE ANALYSIS OF CRIMINAL GROUPS AND PROBLEMATIC gatherings. Geographic analysis allows you to think and communicate "visually" about the problem you are investigating. This can be very helpful in your process of research, analysis, and presentation of the intelligence you have gathered. It can help you provide your police department with timely and accurate intelligence, and also with advice on tactics and deployment strategies.

The questions you might seek to answer using GIS include the following:

- Where are these groups concentrated geographically?

- How dispersed are they in your jurisdiction, state, nationally, or even internationally?

- Can the environmental characteristics of the place where these groups are found give you any additional clues about the group?

- Which kinds of urban areas or cities are these groups more likely to operate in?

- Are there any unique geographic features of the area that hold some special meaning for the groups who live there?

- Have there been geographic shifts in the groups' movements throughout years? If so, what dictates these geographic shifts?

- Can you identify any geographic patterns about the movements or distributions of these groups throughout your jurisdiction, the state, or the nation?

- What targets are most at risk? Where are these targets located?

Geographic analysis and problem-oriented policing

The analysis needed for problem-oriented policing under SARA (Step 4) can also be applied in geographic analysis (see Vann and Darson listed below).

Scanning. Maps can quickly identify crime clusters and hot spots by location, time of day, type of crime, etc. For example, you can use GIS to identify types of crimes committed by the group you are studying. But be cautious. Some problems are not strongly geographical, and will not show up on maps. So do not rely exclusively on maps to detect problems.

Analysis. Maps can be used to relate crime to other spatial variables, such as street layout, transportation arteries, land use categories, locations, and so on. It can also be used to profile crimes that have been committed by the group you are studying, which will give you valuable information on offenders and their characteristics. GIS can also be used to map at-risk targets and locations where these groups operate. In addition, GIS can be used to understand the reasons why the groups commit the crime and how location affects their decision.

Response. Maps can be used strategically (e.g., identifying crime patterns) and tactically (e.g., extrapolating serial crimes to predict anticipated targets). If you have identified at-risk targets and locations, for example, GIS can be used to map the response strategy you are proposing to your department, thus allowing for well-planned resource allocation.

Assessment. Maps can be used as before and after overviews depicting the effects of the intervention proposed. Such examination will allow you to make an assessment of the success or the failure of the intervention implemented.

Cracking down on gangs with GIS

The Akron (Ohio) Police Department's Gang Unit incorporated mapping in their efforts to address the gang problem in the city. The unit used graffiti markings throughout the city to identify the active gangs and to record gang boundaries and track gang activity. Gang Unit officers began by visiting the sites and taking pictures of the graffiti, which were marked with the graffiti's location. The data was then entered into a GIS database to map the boundaries of more than 30 gangs in Akron. Apart from allowing officers to describe the areas where gang activity was present, this also enabled them to identify overlapping space—"hot zones" or "conflict zones"—where gang conflict was most common. These areas were identified through graffiti portraying insults between the rival gangs. The map of these territories is shown in Figure 9 on page 51.

Tracking gang activity in Orange County, California

Recognizing that gang activity crossed jurisdictional boundaries, the Orange County Chiefs and Sheriffs Association created a countywide Gang Strategy Steering Committee to address the shared problem of gang violence. The committee comprised 22 law enforcement agencies, as well as researchers, local government agencies, the community, and businesses. It created a Gang Incident Tracking System (GITS), which was used, in conjunction with GIS, for mapping and spatial analysis of gang activity in the county. GITS and GIS were used not only for monthly statistics and information management, but also for personnel deployment, strategic planning, and resource management. The data gathered through these systems was used to evaluate gang prevention strategies, and intervention and suppression activities for each individual department, as well as for the county.

Geospatial analysis of terrorist activities

Researcher Brent Smith and colleagues used GIS to examine incidents of terrorism in the United States during the past 25 years. Specifically, the research focused on the planning processes and behaviors that the terrorists engaged in while preparing their attacks. A strong spatial relationship was found between terrorist incidents, terrorists' preparatory behaviors, and where they resided. Fifty percent of incidents happened within 30 miles from where they resided, and this was most apparent among international, left-wing, and single-issue terrorists. The analysis also found, for example, that in the case of environmental terrorists, antecedent activities took place very close to the incident location, with a median distance of about 5.3 miles. For international terrorists, this distance ranged between 271 and 810 miles, implying a quite different planning strategy.

The **Crime Mapping and Analysis Program (CMAP)** provides training to law enforcement agencies in the use of GIS, as well as crime and intelligence mapping. The program is funded by the National Institute of Justice's Office of Science and Technology. CMAP provides useful resources including a crime analysis unit developer kit, free software downloads, publications, and free crime mapping and analysis manuals. Their website is www.justnet.org/Pages/cmap.aspx.

READ MORE:

Spencer Chainey and Jerry Ratcliffe. 2005. *GIS and Crime Mapping.* New York: Wiley.

Brent L. Smith, Jackson Cothren, Paxton Roberts, and Kelly R. Damphousse. 2008. *Geospatial Analysis of Terrorist Activities: The Identification of Spatial and Temporal Patterns of Preparatory Behavior of International and Environmental Terrorists.* Report published by the U.S. Department of Justice under Grant #2005-IJ-CX-0200. www.ncjrs.gov/pdffiles1/nij/grants/222909.pdf.

Irvin Vann and David Garson. 2003. *Crime Mapping: New Tools for Law Enforcement.* New York: Peter Lang Publishing.

Figure 9. Major gang territories in South Akron

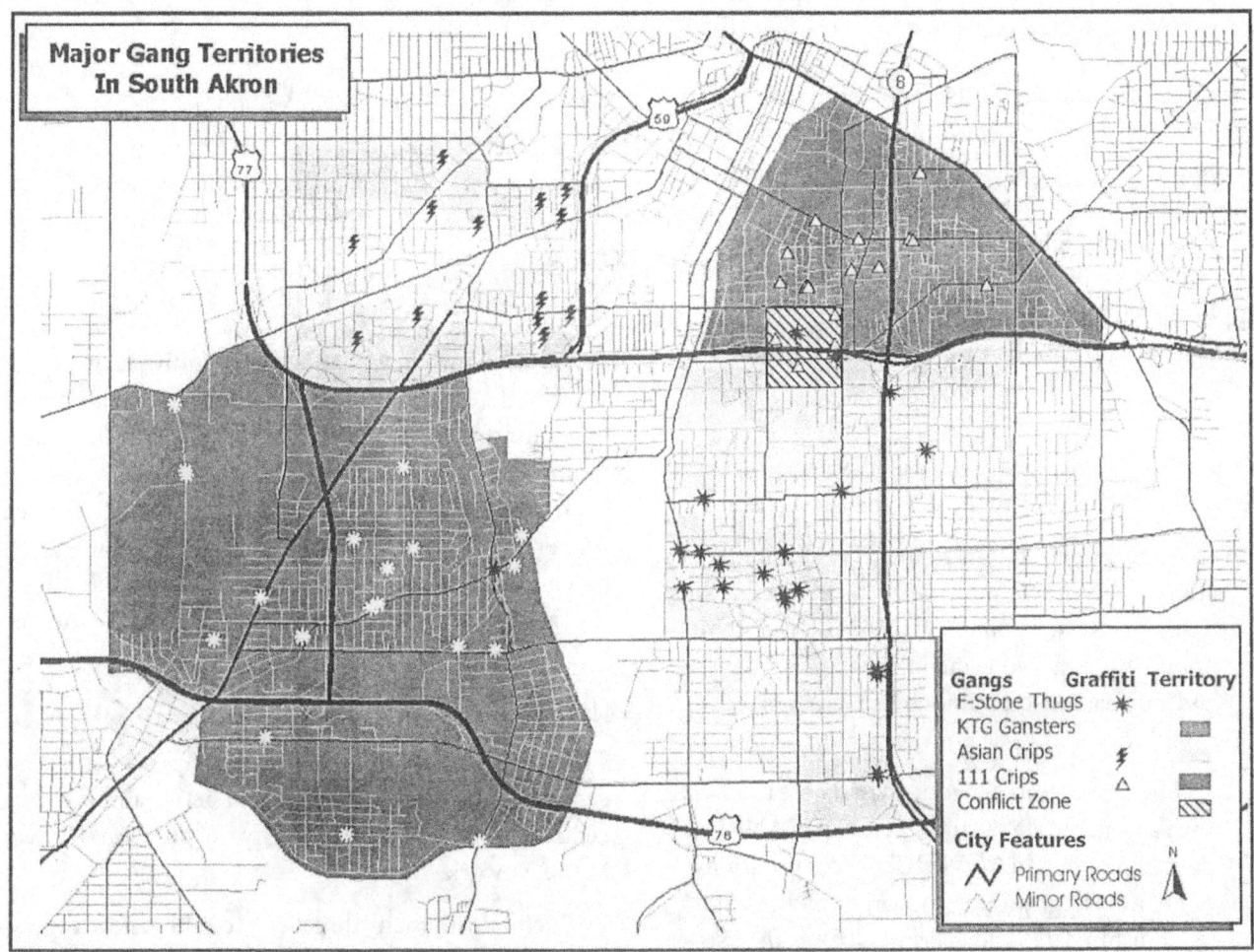

Source: Otto et al. n.d. *Cracking Down on Gangs with GIS.* Akron (Ohio) Police Department.
(Available at faculty.uml.edu/apattavina/44.594/GISGangs.pdf.)

19

NETWORK ANALYSIS ALLOWS YOU TO EXAMINE LINKS BETWEEN MEMBERS OF A GROUP AND RELATIONSHIPS among groups and organizations. It has been applied to investigations of organized crime groups and street gangs, and in uncovering terrorist networks.

It is often important to determine each individual's role within the group. For example, when investigating an organized crime group, you can integrate information from other sources, such as crime incident data, telephone records, and surveillance reports to determine who the leader is; who is responsible for drug supply, distribution, sales, smuggling; who handles money laundering; and so on.

Types of network analysis

Researchers categorize network analysis into three generations according to the degree of complexity:

1. The first generation is a manual approach. It creates a link chart showing criminal associations based on raw data on relationships. This might not be difficult to do when the group is small and the relationships among its members are not complex.

2. Second generation network analysis uses software, such as Analyst's Notebook, Netmap, XANALYS Link Explorer, and COPLINK. These programs can handle large groups and large amounts of relationship data. They permit a visual analysis of relationships among members of the groups and are helpful in determining whether the group is loosely or tightly organized.

3. Third generation social network analysis provides a graphic representation of social networks (also known as a sociogram) and can reveal subgroups, discover patterns of interaction, identify central individuals, and uncover network organization and structure. Because it uses mathematical computations to identify these patterns, it allows less subjectivity on the part of the analyst and reduces the risk of omitting important details. This type of network analysis is becoming widely used by researchers and analysts.

Elements of social network analysis

Key elements to analyze when performing social network analysis include actors, network positions, network structure, network density, and connectedness.

Actors

When studying particular actors or individuals, you should concentrate on gathering information on connections among individuals, places, vehicles, phone numbers, and other things. Personal characteristics of actors are far less important. The fact that Fred often calls Gene's phone, and Gene was seen driving a car owned by Trisha is more important than the fact that Fred is 25 and Gene is 27, and that no one knows Trisha's age.

Network position

Three major concepts in network analysis—degree centrality, closeness centrality, and betweenness centrality—will help you identify the position of actors in the network:

1. Actors with many direct ties to others have high scores on **degree centrality**. They may play an active role in the network, making them more critical.

2. Actors who are physically closer to more actors in the network will have high scores on **closeness centrality**. They are able to easily coordinate tasks and transfer resources within the network.

3. Lastly, those actors who connect many other actors have high scores on **betweenness centrality**. Their removal may prevent contacts between other actors; effectively fracturing the network.

The Royal Canadian Mounted Police use a *Target Profile Sheet* to gather information about actors involved in serious and organized crime.

Personal Data:

- Personal details
- Information on the target's affiliations (e.g., geographic scope of criminal activity, memberships, or addictions)

Criminal History:

- Target's criminal history
- Target's criminal reputation (e.g., position, influence, and importance in the criminal network)

Criminal Roles:

- The criminal capacity of the actor (e.g., crime projects the actor facilitated)
- The current role or primary function of the actor within the network, and how easily replaced

Skills and Experience:

- The expertise and skills that distinguish this actor from others in the group

Finances:

- Known fixed assets and income of the actor and his/her deemed nominees

Vulnerabilities:

- What personal, behavior, status, or relationship aspects make the actor vulnerable or attractive to law enforcement

Social Ties:

- Connections (including family ties), specified by:
  a. The type of the relationship
  b. Frequency of interaction
  c. Degree of criminal association
  d. Degree of licit professional association
  e. The nature of the social relation

The Investigative Research:

- The investigation itself (previous and ongoing efforts)

Network structure

When analyzing the relationships between two or more actors in the group, you are interested in not only the relationships among them, but also cliques or groups of close ties between these actors. That is, you are examining the structure of the entire network—for example, whether it is loosely or tightly organized. This could be important when devising a response strategy. For instance, more open or widely spread networks are more vulnerable to disruption by removing key members.

Network density

The density of a network allows you to determine how close knit or loose knit it is. Figure 10 gives a simple formula for density and applies it to three networks. The first network has less than a third of the maximum possible connections. The second network has all possible connections. Networks that are fully connected (density of 100 percent) are called cliques. The third network is called a cluster because it is at least 80 percent connected. Note that in the first network, three members (E, F, and G) form a clique. In a clique it may be difficult to distinguish between critical and peripheral members.

Connectedness

You may find it useful to determine the degree of connectedness among members, especially when it is vital for you to determine the flow of communication or authority. Connectedness is determined by the direct and indirect ties among the network members (count the connections between two members). In network 1 of Figure 10, one link connects individuals A and B. Two links connect A to D and three to C or E. Four links are needed to get to the other three members.

Network analysis and Operation Ceasefire

David Kennedy and his colleagues made important use of network analysis during Boston's Operation Ceasefire. Members of various criminal justice agencies identified violent gangs and provided information on the gang members. More importantly, they provided information on conflicts among different street gangs, which were translated into sociograms that laid out the gang conflict network (see Figure 11). Gangs not in conflict with other gangs are in the upper right, but are not part of the network.

This seemingly simple information illustrated why particular geographic areas were experiencing high levels of violence. It also revealed which street gangs were most connected within the network and which therefore merited an intervention focus. Finally, it helped to anticipate consequences of interventions by highlighting rival gangs that might attempt to take advantage of law enforcement focus on a particular street gang.

READ MORE:

F.A.J. Ianni, and E. Reuss-Ianni. 1990. "Network Analysis." In *Criminal Intelligence Analysis,* ed. Paul Andrews and Marilyn Peterson, 67–84. Loomis, California: Palmer Enterprises.

David Kennedy, Anthony Braga, and Anne Morrison Piehl. 1997. "The (Un)Known Universe: Mapping Gangs and Gang Violence in Boston." In *Crime Mapping and Crime Prevention,* ed. D. Weisburd and T. McEwen, 219–262. Monsey, New York: Criminal Justice Press.

20 UNDERTAKE CONVERSATIONAL ANALYSIS OF WIRE TAP DATA

CONVERSATIONAL ANALYSIS IS USED TO INVESTIGATE CRIMINAL NETWORKS AND PROSECUTE CRIMINAL CASES. It involves compiling and reviewing telephone conversations between two or more people in a criminal conspiracy. It reveals relationships between these people, the key players in crimes, and each member's role in the network.

Procedures

Conversational analysis has three main stages: (1) collecting and transforming the data; (2) analyzing the data; and (3) reporting findings.

In more complex investigations you might find it helpful to analyze the conversations using an Ask Sam or Folio Views—hypertext software programs that allow for storing, sorting, retrieving, and analyzing textual data (see Mangai Natarajan's study described below). In other cases, it can be helpful to produce a written transcript to aid in the detailed analysis of conversations: looking at what is said, and what is merely implied but left unsaid. There are two types of analysis for this situation.

Micro analysis

This consists of two forms of analysis, phonological analysis and syntactic analysis.

Phonological Analysis examines the sounds used by those speaking and is necessary when recordings are not clear—for example, if you have to clarify whether someone said "I wouldn't take a bribe, would you?" or "I would take a bribe, wouldn't you?"

Syntactic Analysis examines sentence structure and helps to clarify grammatical relationships. For example, when a speaker says "I want you to do it," the 'you' maybe ambiguous, since it can refer to the other party involved in that part of the conversation, or it might include other people as well. When someone says "I want _you_ to do it" he is most likely referring to the primary respondent in the conversation.

Discourse analysis

Discourse analysis is used to analyze the linguistic aspects of conversations. It comprises a variety of sub-analyses.

Topic Analysis seeks to identify who introduces which topics and whether or not the topics are recycled or reintroduced later in the conversation. This information is useful when establishing the speaker's intentions. Topic analysis is also used to establish conversational dominance. For example, when one person introduces 80 percent of the topics in a conversation, this is indicative of an asymmetrical relationship between the participants, and signifies the person is a leader, or an instigator who is trying to get others to do his will.

Project Caviar

The Caviar network was a criminal enterprise engaged in international drug trafficking. Police in Canada, Europe, and South America ran a two-year investigation that led to the dismantling of hashish and cocaine distribution chains spanning these countries. The primary data submitted as evidence in the trials of 22 members of the network was electronically monitored telephone conversations. These were used to identify primary participants and determine how deeply each person was involved in the trafficking operations.

Response Analysis involves examining the responses to topics introduced by others. Topic response options listed below summarize the most common strategies used by listeners when they have been introduced to a topic. They may:

1. Resolve the topic
2. Resolve part of topic
3. Request clarification or amplification of topic
4. Provide off-topic responses
5. Change or redirect the topic
6. Provide vague, ambiguous, or no response
7. Provide clarification that denies or changes the premise of the topic
8. Deny the topic's premise

For example, if the respondent in the conversation says 'uh-huh,' he is not carefully agreeing to whatever has been introduced. Or when a person does not respond, it generally indicates negativity.

Topic-flow analysis organizes topics sequentially, noting the conversational movement among speakers, and marking the success or failure of the speakers in their efforts to achieve their goals. Topics of discussion are generally put into three categories: substantive topics (the goal of the conversation), corollary topics (ways of achieving or arriving at the substantive topics), and transitional topics (formulaic aspects of a conversation, such as greetings and in-between 'small talk' that often provides psychological breaks from the heavier conversation).

Language function analysis identifies functions of the words used. For example, speakers promise, deny, report facts, complain, give opinions, advise, order, and thank, and they use different linguistic tools to achieve these functions—i.e., using language to get things done.

Contrastive analysis compares phrases used in the conversation analyzed—for example, in an investigative report compiled by police officers. Officers commonly paraphrase the suspect's words so that quite a different message is conveyed from what was actually said. Contrastive analysis will, therefore, allow you to compare and contrast these distinctly different sources of data pertaining to the same people.

Uncovering a drug trafficking organization in New York

Mangai Natarajan of John Jay College of Criminal Justice conducted an analysis in 2000 of wiretap records and other prosecution materials to uncover the structure of a large drug trafficking organization in New York City. She sought to determine the roles and status of the individuals within the organization and to chart the hierarchy among its members. She scanned 600 pages of transcripts of 151 telephone conversations, ranging in duration from 2 to 10 minutes, into "Folio Views." Her analysis consisted of five distinct stages:

1. *Conversational count by individuals.* This yielded a count of the number of conversations each individual was involved in, as well the number of other people with whom he or she had telephone contact.

2. *Status analysis.* This involved the use of a coding guide to determine the relative status of individuals. The guide was used to distinguish between people of higher and lower status, and included such indicators as requesting information, expressing satisfaction, providing information, giving orders, clarifying orders, and use of 'sir.'

3. *Task analysis.* This involved identifying the major tasks performed by each individual by inspecting the content of the conversations. The individuals were identified as bosses, assistant managers, field workers reporting to the assistant managers, and field workers reporting to the chief operator.

4. *Network analysis.* This involved establishing links between individuals (Step 19).

5. *The organizational chart.* This involved developing an organizational chart by using the information obtained from stages 1-4. This is shown in Figure 12 on page 58.

Figure 12. Structure of the drug trafficking organization according to wiretap database

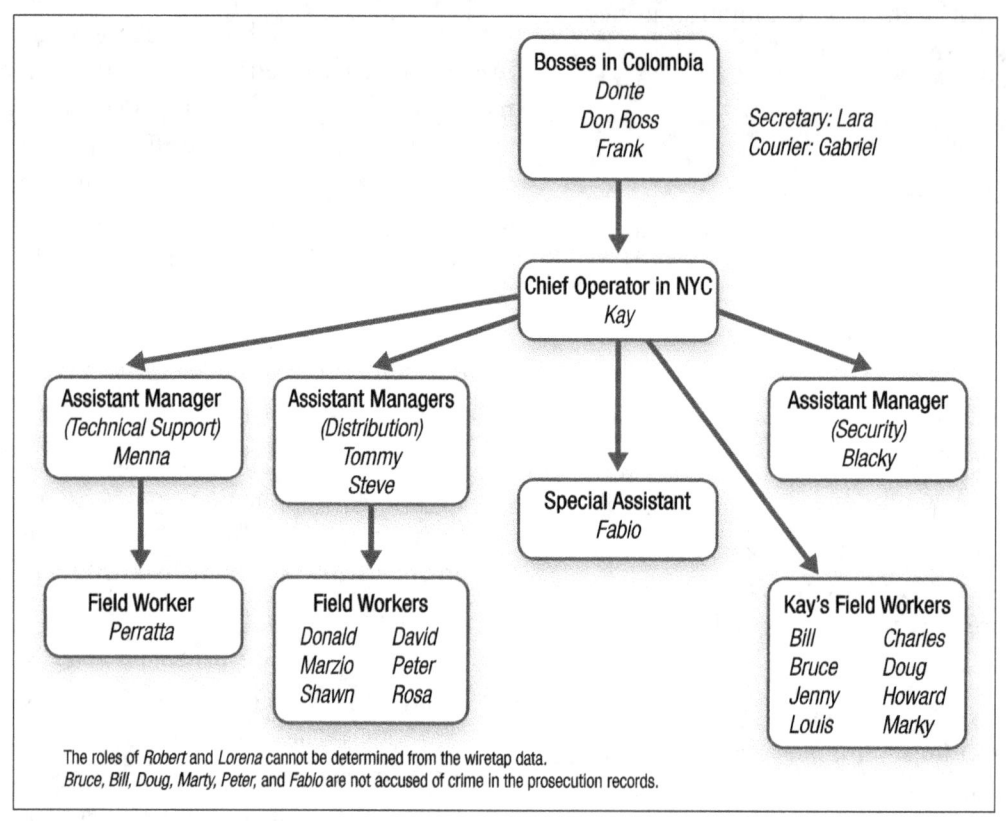

Source: Natarajan 2000.

READ MORE:

Roger Shuy. 1990. "The Analysis of Tape Recorded Conversations." In *Criminal Intelligence Analysis,* ed. Paul Andrews and Marilyn Peterson, 117–147. Loomis, California: Palmer Enterprises.

Mangai Natarajan. 2000. "Understanding the Structure of a Drug Trafficking Organization: A Conversational Analysis." In *Illegal Drug Markets: From Research to Prevention Policy,* ed. Mangai Natarajan and Mike Hough, 273–298. Monsey, New York: Criminal Justice Press.

21 COMPARE COMPETING HYPOTHESES

UNFORTUNATELY, YOUR BEST INTELLIGENCE INFORMATION IS ALWAYS INCOMPLETE, often riddled with errors, sometimes contradictory, and typically ambiguous. This is mostly because you are trying to predict the behaviors of people who are trying to conceal their actions from the police. If your best efforts have a high chance of being wrong, how can you improve your intelligence information?

The answer is to consider alternatives and systematically compare these alternatives. Morgan Jones describes an eight-stage approach, developed by the CIA, called Analysis of Competing Hypotheses (ACH). We will follow his description here.

Stage 1: Generate hypotheses. Typically, there is more than one way to interpret data. So it is better to package the information produced from the data as a set of competing hypotheses: a range of plausible alternative interpretations of the data. Sometimes a single analyst can imagine multiple interpretations. But it is often useful to have several people consider the data and come up with alternatives.

Stage 2: Construct a matrix for comparing the hypotheses. Examples are given in Tables 9, 10, and 11. While you can examine any number of hypotheses, it may be more practical to restrict consideration to the most plausible ones, or to the most contrasting ones (that is, minor variations of the same basic hypotheses are lumped together).

Stage 3: List evidence along the left side. Evidence comes from the data already collected. Focus only on significant evidence, rather than many minor details that could be distracting and irrelevant. Also, if the

absence of information is important, then this too, is evidence. This will be particularly significant if a hypothesis asserts that certain information should be available, but it cannot be found. Also ask, "What evidence not in the matrix would overturn the hypothesis, if it were available?" Looking for this evidence can help evaluate these hypotheses.

Stage 4: Test evidence for consistency with each hypothesis. Once you list all the evidence, work across (row by row) and determine if each piece of evidence is consistent with each hypothesis. If the evidence is consistent with a hypothesis, put a **C** in the cell for the hypothesis. If it is inconsistent, put an **I** in the cell. And enter ? in the cell if it is unclear whether the evidence is consistent or inconsistent with a hypothesis. If you wish, you can give degrees of consistency or inconsistency using numbers, symbols, or colors.

Stage 5: Refine the matrix. You may find new hypotheses that had not been considered. These should be added. New evidence may be uncovered and this should be added. Block out any piece of evidence that is consistent with all hypotheses (as is the case with evidence one in Table 10: Matrix 2). Evidence that is consistent with all hypotheses cannot help you determine which hypotheses are the most likely to be true. Do not discard this evidence, as it may turn out to be useful later.

Stage 6: Evaluate each hypothesis. Now, work down and consider each hypothesis separately. Block out any hypothesis for which there is considerable inconsistent evidence. Before making a final decision, consider the quality of the evidence involved. In Table 11: Matrix 3, we have blocked out hypotheses **A** and **C** because three of the four relevant pieces of evidence are inconsistent with them.

Table 9. Matrix 1

MATRIX 1: Testing each piece of evidence for consistency				
Evidence	Hypotheses			
	A	B	C	D
1.	C	C	C	C
2.	I	C	I	C
3.	I	?	I	I
4.	I	C	C	C
5.	I	C	I	I

Based on Morgan 1998

Stage 7: Rank the remaining hypotheses. The hypothesis that is rated the highest has the *least inconsistent evidence*. Hypothesis **B** appears superior to hypothesis **D** in Matrix 3, because it has no inconsistent evidence, though one piece of evidence is ambiguous. Because the data on which the evidence is built can be subject to alternative interpretations, different analysts may have different interpretations. The advantage of the ACH process is that it forces everyone involved to look at all the hypotheses and evidence systematically. It can eliminate the hypotheses that are least likely and narrow the discussion to a few hypotheses. If, at this step, you determine that specific types of data could break the deadlock, then commission additional data collection. When new evidence is available, go back to step 5 and compare the remaining hypotheses with the old and new evidence.

Stage 8: Perform a sanity check. Morgan advocates reviewing the findings to make sure no mistakes were made and that those involved are comfortable with the decision.

Though you can conduct the ACH process with paper and pencil, the Palo Alto Research Center (PARC) has developed a simple and free downloadable software program. The PARC software has several additional features. It allows you to describe the type of evidence, rate the credibility of the evidence, and rate the relevance of the evidence. It also allows you to give a score to the evidence for each hypothesis and come up with a numerical score for each hypothesis. Finally, though the PARC software has somewhat different steps, the underlying logic is the same as the steps described here.

It is important to remember that ACH relies on the logic of refutation rather than support. In other words, *ACH systematically eliminates the worst hypotheses* (those which are least consistent with the evidence). In this way it narrows the field of plausible hypotheses. It does not prove a hypothesis is true. The hypotheses remaining are the least inconsistent; least bad.

Table 10. Matrix 2

MATRIX 2: Eliminating evidence consistent with all hypotheses				
Evidence	Hypotheses			
	A	B	C	D
1.	C	C	C	C
2.	C	C	I	C
3.	I	?	I	I
4.	I	C	C	C
5.	I	C	I	I

Based on Morgan 1998

Table 11. Matrix 3

MATRIX 2: Eliminating evidence consistent with all hypotheses				
Evidence	Hypotheses			
	A	B	C	D
1.	C	C	C	C
2.	C	C	I	C
3.	I	?	I	I
4.	I	C	C	C
5.	I	C	I	I

Based on Morgan 1998

Though ACH cannot assure that intelligence information is always correct, by forcing a systematic rigorous approach to using data it reduces the chances of error.

READ MORE:

Morgan Jones. 1998. *The Thinker's Tool Kit: 14 Powerful Techniques for Problem Solving.* New York: Three Rivers Press.

Palo Alto Research Center. 2006. *ACH$_{2.0.3}$Download Page—Analysis of Competing Hypotheses.* www2.parc.com/istl/projects/ach/ach.html.

Michael Townsley, Monique Mann, and Kristian Garrett. 2011. The Missing Link of Crime Analysis: A Systematic Approach to Testing Competing Hypotheses. *Policing* 5(2): 158–171.

RIGHT AT THE BEGINNING OF THIS MANUAL, WE MENTIONED THAT THE 9/11 COMMISSION CRITICIZED INTELLIGENCE agencies for failing to "connect the dots" and that this criticism focused attention on the need to find ways of sharing critical information. As former CIA director, R. James Woolsey, noted in testimony to Congress, "the flow of information sharing is likely to be more from localities to Washington, rather than the other way around." The fact that local police came face-to-face with three of the 9/11 hijackers in traffic stops before the attack is often cited as an example of an opportunity that was lost because an integrated information sharing system was not in place.

We are still struggling with the difficulties of putting such a system in place. The regional Joint Terrorism Task Forces established by the FBI throughout the country before 9/11, represent one attempt to find a solution to this problem. Fusion in many states represents another information-sharing initiative. Information from multiple jurisdictions is pooled and made available to participating police. A center's mission can be limited to antiterrorism, but it often includes other significant crimes, such as insurance fraud, money laundering, and armed robbery. Therefore, these fusion centers can serve as a valuable resource for your department.

Joint Terrorism Task Forces

There are now more than 100 JTTFs throughout the country, including the 56 FBI field offices. Their mission is to coordinate federal, state, and local law enforcement efforts to detect, prevent, and respond to terrorist attacks. Primarily investigative and analytic agencies, JTTF are staffed by FBI investigators, agents from federal agencies—such as the Bureau of Alcohol, Tobacco, Firearms and Explosives (ATF) and the Bureau of Immigration and Customs Enforcement (ICE)—and detectives from local police and sheriff's departments. Several successes have been credited to the JTTF, including the arrest and conviction of the terrorists who mounted the first attack on the World Trade Center in 1993 and of the so-called shoe bomber, Richard Reid.

Impediments to information sharing

In Step 15 we discussed some of the impediments to sharing information among the personnel of a single police department. Here we list six important impediments to sharing information among different departments and jurisdictions:

1. There are more than 17,000 state and local law enforcement agencies in the United States, very few of which have staff trained in a common intelligence curriculum and technology to collate, analyze, and exploit raw intelligence data. Even within the same force, there might be little interconnectivity among existing computer systems.

2. Secrecy is the stock-in-trade of intelligence agencies; historically, protecting sources and preventing leaks has been of great importance. This is why the need-to-know doctrine drives policy on information sharing. Unfortunately, in practice this doctrine inhibits information sharing and, therefore, inhibits new insights that sometimes occur when new eyes examine old information.

3. Particularly in the early stages of an inquiry, it is likely that investigators will guard their information jealously. There are two reasons for this:

   a. Investigators may be wary of leaks that would jeopardize the investigation. They may know that officers in other forces might benefit from the information, but who might also treat it carelessly or misuse it. Consequently, they might not share information when they should have done.

b. Investigators (understandably) wish to reap the kudos that will result from successfully apprehending the criminals they have been investigating. Sharing the information with some other enforcement agency, particularly one higher in prestige, could result in that agency taking over the investigation, making the arrests, and gaining all the glory.

4. Some crimes, such as terrorism, are rare and it is hard for people to remain vigilant when nothing seems to be happening, and hard to maintain the morale of those doing the watching. Added to this is that useless information is vastly more common than information that is useful. While we often hear stories of intelligence successes, resulting from tips received or surveillance undertaken, we do not hear about the work that leads nowhere. This lack of success can result in a "why bother" attitude and a reluctance to expend the effort needed in pursuing investigations. It also can mean that investigators are reluctant to lose face by sharing information that could prove to be useless.

5. The essence of prevention is stopping something from happening. It can be hard to demonstrate that such efforts have been successful when the agency that collects the relevant information is not the agency that takes the action to prevent the thing from happening. Once again, this fact works against the intelligence function and more specifically against the sharing of information.

6. Finally, there is much misunderstanding of laws and regulations governing the sharing of intelligence. In discussions on this topic someone is sure to bring up 28 C.F.R. Part 23, which only applies to federally-funded multi-jurisdictional intelligence systems, and even then only has very general rules about data access and storage. Many police and analysts seem to think that it prohibits them from sharing data or requires them to do certain things it does not actually require. So try to clarify legal/regulatory impediments that do and do not apply in your particular case.

What, then, should you do to promote information sharing? There are two principles that should guide your approach:

1. Identify key individuals within in or near your jurisdiction, who could be a continuing source of useful information, and cultivate a relationship with them so that they get to know and trust you.

2. When a dealing with a specific problem (for example, one of a criminal motorcycle gang or a pedophile ring) you should identify specific stakeholders with a direct interest in reducing the problem, who would be likely to help you with your investigation.

READ MORE:

Graeme Newman and Ronald Clarke. 2008. *Policing Terrorism: An Executive's Guide.* Washington, D.C.: U.S. Department of Justice, Office of Community Oriented Policing Services.

OFFENDING IS NOT AN INSTANTANEOUS EVENT THAT OCCURS WITHOUT A PAST OR A FUTURE. It is a process that offenders must complete for their crime to be successful. This step and the following one will show you how to diagram such processes so you can disrupt them.

Follow a four-stage procedure for linking the process that offender groups follow in committing crimes to a set of interventions designed to thwart the group's abilities.

1. Describe the process offenders follow to commit crimes.

2. Add other actors and describe their actions that facilitate the crime.

3. Develop possible prevention interventions at each process stage, for each actor.

4. Select a comprehensive set of actions from these possible actions.

Describe the process

The simplest crime process diagram has three stages that describe what the offenders do before they can commit a crime, during the commission, and afterwards (top row in Figure 13). All preparatory actions, such as finding crime targets, planning, finding weapons and other tools, organizing confederates, and so forth, are in the before stage. In the during stage are all the actions the offenders must take while directly carrying out the crime, including overwhelming victims, gaining access to the site, providing security, and securing valuables. The last stage includes activities such as escaping, disposing of stolen items, threatening witnesses, and laundering money.

Any of the stages can be divided into multiple sub-stages to show the process in greater detail (see second row of Figure 13, and for more detail see Step 11).

Figure 13. Crime process diagrams

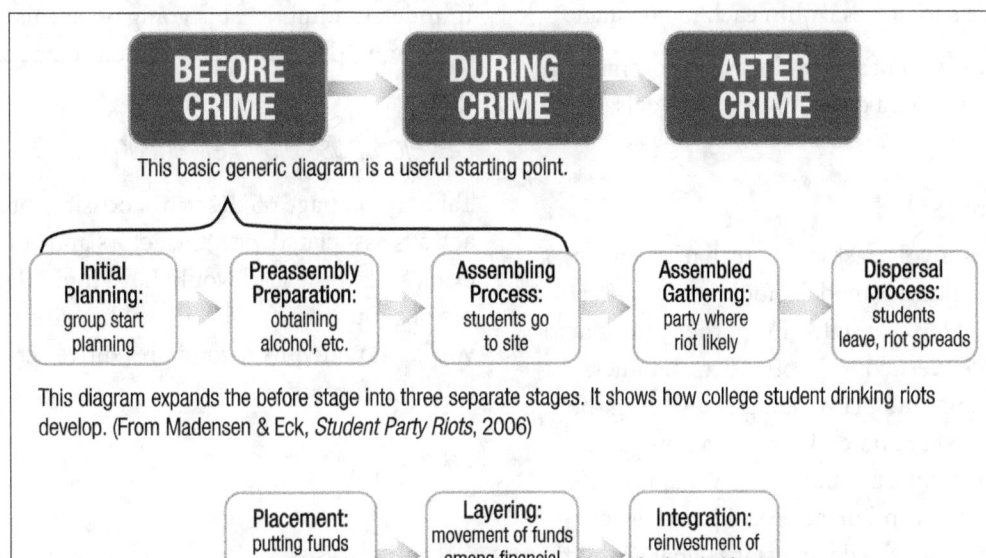

Table 12. Adding details to the model

INTELLIGENCE SUMMARY GRID				
WHEN	**ACTORS**			
	Group A	Group B	Targets	Place managers
Long Before				What place managers are doing at this stage
Just Before		What this group is doing at this stage		
During	What this group is doing at this stage			
After			What targets are doing at this stage	
Comments:				
In this example, there are two interacting offender groups, their crime targets, and people who own or manage locations critical for the crime. Other combinations of actors are possible, as are different stages of the process. In each cell, describe what the actor is doing at that stage, based on intelligence. For groups, describe what they do to carry off the crime successfully. For targets, describe what they do, or fail to do, to protect themselves. If a cell is empty there is a lack of data.				

The before-during-after framework is useful, but it does not fit all crimes. Money laundering, for example, follows a different process. The model of money laundering in the bottom of the figure is very general. A model for a specific money laundering operation would describe sub-stages within each major stage.

If the offender group has several ways to commit the crime, then you should create multiple models: one for each way.

Add other actors

Since all crimes involve actors other than offenders, a comprehensive process model should account for their actions, too. In Step 7 we introduced the various actors we should be concerned with: offenders, handlers, targets, guardians, and place managers. During the before stage, what are potential victims doing that the offenders can take advantage of? What is being done by the owners and managers of places where the crimes occur? At the during stage, what are all the actors doing? And afterwards, what are all the relevant actors doing?

Table 12 shows how this additional data can be included. The relevant actors depend on the crime problem, as does the number of stages. Empty cells indicate where there is too little intelligence data to determine what a particular actor is doing. If understanding what is going on at this stage is important, then you need to focus data gathering on this cell.

Develop possible interventions

Table 13 on page 65 describes possible prevention actions associated with the actors and stage. Ideally, every cell in the grid would have multiple possible actions. But some cells will be blank indicating that you cannot identify a good preventive action due to a lack of information.

Table 13. Developing responses

INTELLIGENCE SUMMARY GRID				
WHEN	ACTORS			
	Group A	Group B	Targets	Place managers
Long Before	Preventive actions			Preventive actions
Just Before		Preventive actions		
During			Preventive actions	
After	Preventive actions			
Comments:				
In each cell create a list of actions involving that actor who could disrupt the crime process at that stage. Ideally, the entire grid would be filled, but this requires intelligence for each cell. Blank cells indicate where no prevention will be implemented because of lack of intelligence. Once a comprehensive list of actions has been developed, select the combination of actions most likely to be implemented and most likely to have an impact on the problem.				

Select a set of interventions

Having created a list of possible prevention actions, organized by actor and stage, it is time to select the combination of actions that are most productive. The characteristics of a good set of interventions can be described by the acronym EAGLE. The parts are:

- Effective
- Acceptable to the community
- Go well together
- Legal
- Expected to be implemented

To create a comprehensive set of prevention actions; 1) address each stage of the process, and 2) address at least two actors at each stage. This provides a layered attack on the offender group's capabilities that has built-in redundancy. Should some actions fail, or should the offender group attempt to thwart the prevention, other parts of the plan can take up the slack.

READ MORE:

Derek Cornish. 1994. "The Procedural Analysis of Offending and its Relevance for Situational Prevention." Vol. 3 of *Crime Prevention Studies*. Monsey, New York: Criminal Justice Press.

COMPLETELY REMOVING THE OFFENDER GROUP MAYBE DESIRABLE, BUT NOT BE POSSIBLE because of offender replacement (Step 13). If members of the group are arrested, new members may replace them. Or new groups can spring up to continue the offending. This is often the case with violent street groups and retail drug dealing organizations. It is also the case with large-scale international criminal organizations. Another circumstance under which removal strategies may be inadequate occurs when removal can provoke violence. Consequently, you need to use other approaches that are complementary with a removal strategy but help thwart replacement and violent competition.

Situational Crime Prevention can be very useful for influencing offender behavior, particularly when offender removal is difficult, replacement is likely, or removal creates additional violence. As we described in Step 6, offenders make choices based on the local context of crime opportunities; they exploit the environment, taking advantage of circumstances that encourage crime. Recall ESEER: if crime is easy, safe, excusable, enticing, and rewarding there will be more crime. Situational Crime Prevention changes the incentives. It alters the social and physical context of crime to make crime harder or riskier, or by removing rewards, excuses, and provocations.

Because different crimes are encouraged by different features of the environment, you need to analyze local circumstances to determine exactly how to influence offenders. To aid the selection of appropriate interventions, a classification of 25 situational techniques has been developed, which is reproduced in Figure 14. We will briefly summarize the 25 techniques below.

Increase the Effort. Target hardening involves securing targets. Access control makes it difficult for the offender to get to the target. Exit screening makes it difficult to escape with the target, or from the target site. Deflection (for example, through street closures) steers offenders away from targets. Controlling tools makes the crime harder by denying critical resources (e.g., explosive materials) to the offender group.

Figure 15. Applying situational prevention to the entire crime process

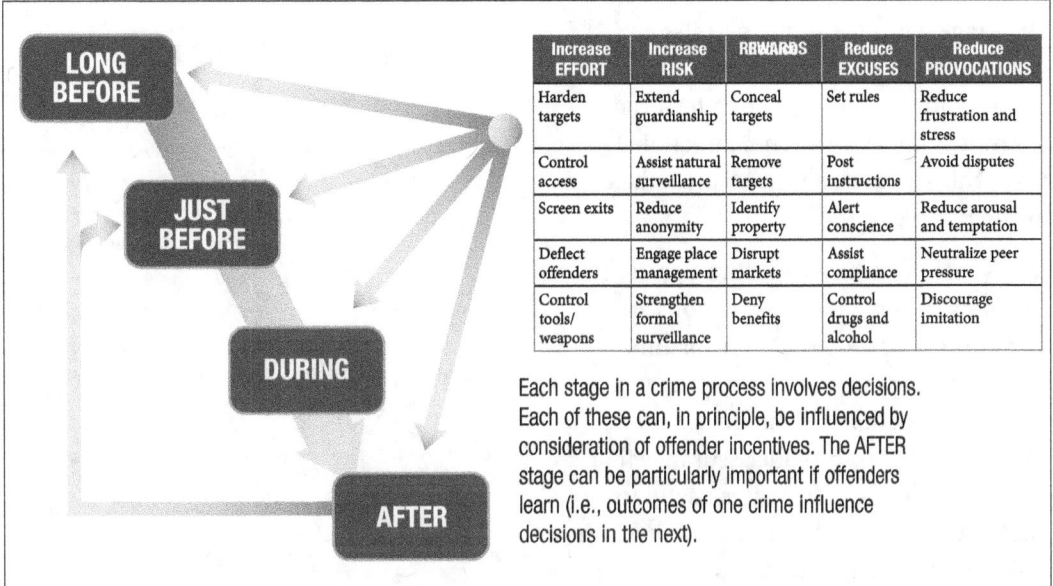

Increase EFFORT	Increase RISK	REWARDS	Reduce EXCUSES	Reduce PROVOCATIONS
Harden targets	Extend guardianship	Conceal targets	Set rules	Reduce frustration and stress
Control access	Assist natural surveillance	Remove targets	Post instructions	Avoid disputes
Screen exits	Reduce anonymity	Identify property	Alert conscience	Reduce arousal and temptation
Deflect offenders	Engage place management	Disrupt markets	Assist compliance	Neutralize peer pressure
Control tools/ weapons	Strengthen formal surveillance	Deny benefits	Control drugs and alcohol	Discourage imitation

Each stage in a crime process involves decisions. Each of these can, in principle, be influenced by consideration of offender incentives. The AFTER stage can be particularly important if offenders learn (i.e., outcomes of one crime influence decisions in the next).

Increase the Risks. Extending guardianship involves having citizens do more to protect each other. Assisting natural surveillance is related to this; it makes it easier for citizens to watch an area. Reducing anonymity reduces the ability of offenders to hide by being unknown. Place management involves a wide variety of practices to engage owners of locations in prevention. Formal surveillance employs dedicated security personnel or electronic monitoring.

Reduce Rewards. Concealing targets attempts to hide them from offenders. Removing targets takes this a step further and takes the targets away completely. Property identification involves marking targets so they have less value at resale. Disrupting markets also makes it difficult to sell stolen merchandise or illegal substances and services. Finally, denying benefits entails taking the value out of the behavior (for example by using ink tags in clothing stores that spoil stolen items).

Remove Excuses. Rule setting removes ambiguity for misbehavior and allows early intervention. Posting instructions serves as a reminder about rules. Awakening conscience appeals to offenders' sense of justice. Assisting compliance makes good behavior more likely. Finally, controls on drugs and alcohol make it harder to overcome inhibitions about committing crime.

Reduce Provocations. Reducing frustration and stress makes it harder for offenders to justify their actions. Avoiding disputes keeps conflicts from arising or getting out of hand. Curtailing emotional arousal also reduces temptations to offend. Neutralizing peer pressure keeps offenders from encouraging each other to commit crimes. Discouraging imitation limits information to offenders so they are less likely to copy criminal behaviors of others.

Some techniques may work better together than separately. Thus, rule setting is typically accompanied by posted instructions that serve as veiled threats to an offender. And rules that require people to reveal their identities both removes anonymity and increases the offenders' perceived risk. No technique works in all circumstances for all crimes. Thus, rule setting and instructions alone may be of little importance to a determined offender, but they may deter the more casual, opportunistic offenders. However, all the techniques have an important role in controlling particular crimes in some circumstances.

As we have discussed, intelligence data can be used to determine the process that the offender group uses to exploit crime opportunities. At each stage of the process a situational analysis should be conducted to determine the best ways to keep the group from successfully executing that part of the process. This is illustrated in Figure 15. While it is obvious that curtailing early stages of the process can prevent the group from committing crimes, it is less obvious why dealing with the final stage is productive. The reason is that it is this stage when the group gets its reward. Whether it is the sales of stolen goods, an enhanced reputation for a killing, or publicity for a terrorist attack, most rewards come at the end. Situational interventions at this stage can substantially reduce the incentive for further crime.

A comprehensive strategy for preventing a group from producing crimes will contain a set of actions at each stage of the group's crime process. While planning a strategy for preventing the group's activities you should describe the situational techniques used at each stage of the process. To provide assurance that the overall strategy will be effective, it is useful to employ at least two different types of techniques (e.g., increasing risks and reducing rewards, or removing excuses and increasing effort) at each stage.

READ MORE:

Ronald Clarke. 2008. "Situational Crime Prevention." In *Environmental Criminology and Crime Analysis,* ed. Richard Wortley and Lorraine Mazerolle. Cullompton, Devon: Willan Publishing.

Marcus Felson and Ronald Clarke. 1998. *Opportunity Makes the Thief.* Police Research Series. Paper 98. London. Home Office

25 WORK WITH GATHERINGS AND CROWDS

IN STEP 17, WE DISCUSSED THE IMPORTANT ROLE THAT COMMUNITY MEMBERS PLAY IN ADDRESSING CRIME. This is particularly true when dealing with large gatherings of individuals, though many of these gatherings are not serious problems for the police. Special events, large block parties, celebrations, and daily commuter crowds typically need the police only to provide traffic regulation, offer directions to citizens, and ensure security against minor crimes. However, demonstrations to protest government policy, to push social or economic agendas, to voice opposition to other political or cultural positions, or to take stands against corporate practices may require active police intelligence analysis before, during, and after the events.

Covert gathering of data about the organizers of the gathering, their intentions, and their plans is tempting, but highly risky because it puts personal liberty in jeopardy. Once revealed, or even suspected, covert gathering of data can undermine the public support for the police.

When dealing with gatherings, intelligence analysis must be considered within an overall police strategy for facilitating individuals' abilities to make their opinions known and carry out constitutionally protected actions, while at the same time preventing violence and other harmful behaviors. Spying on individuals to determine who holds what legitimate beliefs and belongs to what legitimate organization is not permissible in most western democracies. Identifying violent individuals, or individuals who facilitate violence, is a legitimate police activity. The boundary between these two actions is grey, and keeping police actions to the correct side of this boundary is often difficult.

One way to keep police away from this boundary is to get the participants in the gathering to keep order, ostracize troublemakers, and not obstruct focused police actions to remove troublemakers. This may be difficult, but is often easier than imagined because of some basic characteristics of gatherings and crowds, including:

■ **Individuals in crowds are rational.** Individuals do not surrender their rationality when in crowds nor do they lose their capacity to make decisions.

■ **Large gatherings are diverse.** They contain people with many different perspectives and intentions.

1. In most cases, only a tiny fraction is seeking to create trouble. This group will use the larger gathering for their purposes and may attempt to provoke the police into taking forceful actions against the larger gathering, and thus gain the support of the other members of the gathering.

2. Another slightly larger fraction may be willing to facilitate the troublemaking, or join in once it is started. But they are unlikely to act unless the first group provokes the police to over-react.

3. A much larger proportion of the gathering will stand-by, either confused or puzzled, but if seriously provoked may provide tacit support for the first two groups.

4. The greatest number of participants in the gathering will try to distance themselves from the troublemakers by leaving the scene once trouble starts.

■ **People in gatherings have limited information.** They often know little about what is going on around them. Even with a cell phone and text messages, a person in the middle of a gathering is unlikely to know what is going on at the edges, and those at the head of a march will know little about what is going on at the tail.

Table 14. Dialogue policing before, during, and after a demonstration

BEFORE	DURING	AFTER
Ensure police statements to the media build trust with demonstrators	Check that agreements are kept and facilitate new agreements	Avoid potentially provocative statements in media by the police
Create agreements between demonstration organizers and police	Establish active communication links between police and demonstration organizers	Get feedback on police operations from demonstration organizers
Exchange information between police commanders and demonstration organizers	Prevent hazardous incidents or reduce their seriousness	Explain police actions during the demonstration to demonstrators
Create scenarios for the commander	Read mood in crowds and among police	Give feedback to police on behavior of demonstrators
Involve and inform third parties affected by the demonstration	Inform third parties affected by the demonstration	Exchange information with third parties affected by the demonstration

Adapted from: Holgersson and Knutsson 2010

- **People in gatherings influence each other.** Probably the most important influences on members of a gathering are the people in their immediate vicinity. These are often people who accompany them to the gathering, or who they knew before the gathering.

- **Crowd members and police influence each other.** You cannot understand what the crowd will do without considering what the police will do. And much bad behavior by individuals in crowds is in reaction to police actions, and vice versa. When things go very wrong, it is often because some police and some crowd members co-produced disorder.

To the maximum extent possible, police should facilitate legitimate goals of the gathering. This requires building trust with the leaders of the gathering so their help can be enlisted in policing the gathering. Explaining police actions before, during, and after the gathering is critical. So is having an agreed on plan for the event. Also, because few plans can be implemented without changes, there needs to be a way for police and members of the gathering to communicate.

Overt and bidirectional intelligence is important. The Swedish Police have developed a strategy involving "dialogue policing." Trained officers, dressed in civilian clothes, but clearly identified as police officers, work directly with leaders of the gathering. They pass information about the leaders' intents and concerns to the police commander, and the commander's concerns and intent back to the leaders. They do not spy on individuals in the crowd or report specific illegal behavior—that is the job of others in the police. They seek to dispel rumors and provide a way for the police to negotiate with the gathering's leaders, thereby reducing the anxiety of both the police and members of the gathering. If the police need to take forceful action against specific individuals or a small group, the dialogue officer can explain what is taking place and why.

Dialogue policing is an overall strategy of negotiation and discussion that begins at the earliest stages of planning the gathering (see Table 14). In this context the police can learn a great deal about the gathering without resorting to covert actions.

The dialogue officers are not the only way that information is communicated to the gathering by the police, or that the police gather information about the crowd. Throughout the gathering, police assess the mood of the crowd and modify their actions accordingly. Many of their actions are intended to remove excuses for misbehavior, and to not provoke. At the same time police communicate a specific risk to the few individuals who may be intent on violence, and deny them the rewards of being supported by the vast majority of the crowd. By socially separating those intent on violence from the rest of the crowd, the police make it harder for them to use violence to gain their objectives.

READ MORE:

Stefan Holgersson and Johannes Knutsson. 2010. "Dialogue Policing—A Means for Less Crowd Violence?" In *Preventing Crowd Violence,* ed. Johannes Knutsson and Tamara Madensen, 191–216. Boulder, Colorado: Lynne Rienner Publishers.

26

IDENTIFYING HIGHLY ACTIVE OFFENDERS AND THEN GIVING THEM A DIRECT CREDIBLE THREAT OF LEGAL SANCTIONS can substantially reduce their offending. However, offenders working in a group are more difficult to influence because the group's members can exert strong counter pressure. David Kennedy pioneered a three-pronged approach to reducing group violence, called "Pulling Levers," that not only overcomes this group effect, but also turns it to an advantage. It has been successfully applied in a variety of cities and to problems of street level drug dealing.

Much of the violence in poor neighborhoods is the result of disputes between rival street gangs. The dispute may be over a drug transaction, or a real or imagined slight. Group members encourage each other to violence because they believe that this is expected of them by the other members of the group. In fact, it may be that few if any group members prefer violence, but all believe the others do. In Step 6 we described this as "pluralistic ignorance." Group members also justify their behavior by taking an oppositional stance to legitimate authority, particularly the police, and believe wrongly that they are standing up for the community and have their community's support.

Pulling Levers exploits these mistaken beliefs in order to get group members to regulate each other's conduct. It seeks to accomplish this goal in three ways, all requiring direct communication with offenders:

1. **Providing a direct credible threat.** The objective is to hold the entire group responsible for the violent actions of each member. Standard police practice after a killing is to arrest and prosecute only the offenders directly responsible. Other group members who provide a supporting role are left untouched. Also left untouched are group members not directly involved who have outstanding warrants, are in violation of parole conditions, or in other ways vulnerable to criminal justice sanctions. There is an incentive for those not touched by the investigation to provoke other group members to violence. If one group member takes the fall for a killing, then the other group members achieve higher status. Under Pulling Levers, legal pressure is placed on all group members if one of their members is involved in a killing. The risk is thereby spread to the entire group so there is less incentive for members to provoke each other to violence.

To accomplish this, two sets of data are needed:

a. All violent street groups in an area need to be identified and the relationships among these groups need to be established. Some groups will be allied with each other, some will be fighting with others, and some groups may have no contact with others. This information needs to be updated regularly.

b. All members of each group should be identified: who they are, their descriptions, their criminal histories, where they can be found, and other similar information. This information, too, needs to be routinely updated.

The network of group members and the network of groups are used when communicating with offenders. This addresses the problem of violence created by pluralistic ignorance by giving all group members a face saving way of backing away from violent encounters.

2. **Providing a way out of street life.** Whereas the first purpose is to convey a direct deterrent threat, the second is to offer a way out of the gang through job training, substance abuse treatment, and other help. This not only affords a way out for individual members of the group, but it also threatens the integrity of the group itself because the real possibility of a positive exit undermines the shared belief that legitimate society is a source of the group's troubles. So even if relatively few group members take advantage of the offer, the possibility of a way out reinforces the law enforcement threat of the first message.

3. **Demonstrating that the community is against violence.** The third objective is to provide the community with a forum for expressing their strong dislike of violent behavior. Community members, particularly those closest to the group members—family members, former group members, and people working in the streets—communicate a dual message: "You are part of the community and we want you safely back. But we strongly disapprove of your violence which is destroying our community and if you do not change we will support the actions of the police to make you stop." Socially isolating the group removes the excuse that they are acting on the part of the community.

The call out session

"Call out sessions" are widely used. Group members are summoned to a meeting, held in a safe venue in which all three messages are conveyed. While it is impossible to get all of them to attend, the objective is to get some members from each group who can then bring the word back to those who did not attend. In Cincinnati, most call outs were held in a courtroom so members in jail, as well as those on parole or probation could get the message.

The police deliver the first message, often supported by federal and local prosecutors and other criminal justice agencies. Outreach workers who can guide group members into job training, rehabilitation, or educational services deliver the second message. Community members deliver the third message.

The first meeting seldom achieves a reduction in violence, but the police and other criminal justice agencies must swiftly carry out their threat when the next killing occurs. Then a second call out meeting is held and the results of the investigation are used to demonstrate that the consequences are real. The other two messages are reinforced and the successes of anyone who took advantage of the exit services are highlighted. This cycle sometimes needs to be repeated several times.

It is important to track the progress of these efforts. Much of the analytical support needed to develop network diagrams and track progress for the Cincinnati Initiative to Reduce Violence (CIRV) is provided by the University of Cincinnati's School of Criminal Justice, which routinely monitors shootings and killings in the city and uses group related homicide trends as a method of monitoring effectiveness.

READ MORE:

Anthony Braga, David M. Kennedy, Anne M. Piehl, and Elin J. Waring. 2001. "Measuring the Impact of Operation Ceasefire." In *Reducing Gun Violence: The Boston Gun Project's Operation Ceasefire.* Washington, D.C.: National Institute of Justice. www.ncjrs.gov/pdffiles1/nij/188741.pdf.

University of Cincinnati Policing Institute. 2009. *Implementation of the Cincinnati Initiative to Reduce Violence (CIRV): Year 2 Report.* Cincinnati, Ohio: University of Cincinnati Policing Institute. www.cincinnati-oh.gov/police/pages/-32719-/.

27

IT IS OFTEN DIFFICULT TO DETERMINE IF INTELLIGENCE WORK IS PRODUCTIVE, particularly when it serves a long-term initiative to address criminal groups. Its particular contribution as part of such an initiative is also hard to determine. Like all police functions, however, accountability is critical and all intelligence-driven operations should have clear goals and defined outcomes that can be measured.

The single biggest difficulty is that long-term initiatives tend to lose sight of their goals and begin to focus on their activities. When addressing criminal gangs, for example, the emphasis tends to be on numbers of arrests and disrupting the gangs, rather than reducing the harms the gangs are producing. Intelligence analysts can play an important role in keeping the initiative focused on its goals by measuring outcomes and results. This step examines how to incorporate effectiveness measures into the planning of an intelligence-driven initiative. The principles we describe here are not unique to intelligence, but are, in fact, good practice for all policing.

Setting clear goals and developing measures of effectiveness begins early in the planning of any initiative designed to address group-related crime. Intelligence has an important role to play in both setting goals and developing measures of success. That is, you need to determine how you and others will know whether or not the initiative obtained its objectives.

Table 15 lists four minimal requirements for planning an initiative to address a criminal group. Next to each is its accountability measure. The first thing to be decided is what the initiative is supposed to achieve. These are the goals of the initiative. Goals should be described relative to the harms the group produces. **Goals can be stated in terms of absolute numbers or in percent reductions from current levels.** For example, the Cincinnati Initiative to Reduce Violence

Table 15. Planning and measuring

PLAN	MEASURE	WHAT THE MEASURE SHOWS	WHAT THE MEASURE DOES NOT SHOW
Goals: desired level of problem	**Outcomes:** degree of goal achievement	Whether the initiative is effective in curbing the problems created by the criminal group	Whether the benefit is worth the costs **Efficiency:** To measure efficiency divide outcomes by expenditures or by activities
Objectives: anticipated impacts on the group or their environments	**Results:** degree to which objectives were achieved	Whether the initiative is altering the groups' functioning	Problem reduction effectiveness Compare outcomes to results to see if results are productive
Actions: activities planned	**Activities:** actions carried out	What the initiative is doing	Whether the initiative is achieving anything Compare activities to results to determine achievements
Resources: personnel, equipment, information systems, and money needed	**Expenditures:** resources consumed	The costs of the initiative	Whether these costs are "buying" anything of value See efficiency measurement above

(CIRV, as described in Step 26) set goals in terms of percent reductions in group-related homicides to be achieved over a 12-month period.

An intelligence initiative addressing possible violence associated with a political demonstration could set the goal in terms of property damage, injuries, or other harms that should be minimized. The goal ought to be achievable and meaningful. While completely eliminating group-related homicides is certainly desirable, it may not be achievable. A very small reduction may be achievable, but is less meaningful. The expression, "do not let the perfect be the enemy of the good" applies here. An unattainable perfect goal may prevent the achievement of a very good goal.

The outcome of the initiative is the actual measured reduction in harm. **Outcomes are measures showing how close you came to achieving the planned goals.** It would be the actual number of homicides (or actual percent reduction) in the CIRV example. It would be the actual number of injuries or level of property damage in the example of the political demonstration. Outcomes do not describe the efficiency of the initiative. To determine the "bang for the buck" or "value for money," you need to divide the outcome (e.g., crimes reduced) by the resources used (e.g., money expended). Ideally, each unit of the outcome (e.g., homicide prevented) is associated with a low cost.

Objectives describe the impact of the initiative on the group or the facilitating environment. The initiative seeks to change either the group itself—e.g., break up the group, impede its ability to recruit new members, and so forth—or it seeks to change the environment that facilitates the group's crimes—e.g., deny the group access to specific locations, keep the group's members from intimidating community members, and so forth. The theory of your initiative is that if these objectives can be obtained, then this will lead to achieving your goals.

Results are measures of the degree to which these objectives have been obtained. Because group functioning might not be easily observed, results are often documented through interviews with arrested group members, discussions with community members, informant reports, and from similar sources. Regardless of how successful the initiative is in obtaining desirable results, the impact on the group only matters if the harm from the group's activities can be reduced (outcomes). Results do not measure initiative effectiveness (that is what the outcomes measure), but they show possible progress in that direction.

The next stage down from objectives is actions. The planned **actions are the steps necessary to produce the desired objectives.** Examples of such actions are drug buys, surveillance of group members, interviews with victims, and meetings with community members.

Counting the actions carried out, or measuring the time expended on actions produces measures of activities. Activity measures show what you did (but not what you accomplished). Knowing what the initiative does is important so activities can be linked to results, and then outcomes. But activities consume resources so it is not desirable to maximize activities unless they produce commensurate results and outcomes. Ideally, you would have very few activities and produce great results and major outcomes.

Having determined what actions are necessary to carry out the initiative, the final step is to determine the resources needed to carry out the actions. **Resources are the raw inputs into the initiative.** Typically, the personnel constitute the bulk of resources, while specialized equipment and databases are also often needed.

Expenditures measure resources used, such as personnel time spent on various tasks, informant payments, and fees for access to proprietary databases. It is often useful to monetize expenditures so you can create efficiency measures by dividing outcomes by money expended. A highly efficient initiative achieves large outcomes with little expenditure, while an inefficient initiative costs a great deal and gains little.

In short, expenditures buy activities, which produce results, which create outcomes. This is depicted in Figure 16. While the planning process starts with goals, moves to objectives, then to actions, and ends with resources, the measurement process tracks the actual implementation of the initiative, and works in the opposite direction: from expenditures, to activities, to results, and ends with outcomes.

Tracking these four types of measures over time is critical for ensuring that the initiative is doing what it is supposed to do. If the outcomes are not improving then changes need to be made in the planned objectives and actions.

Figure 16. Measurement schema

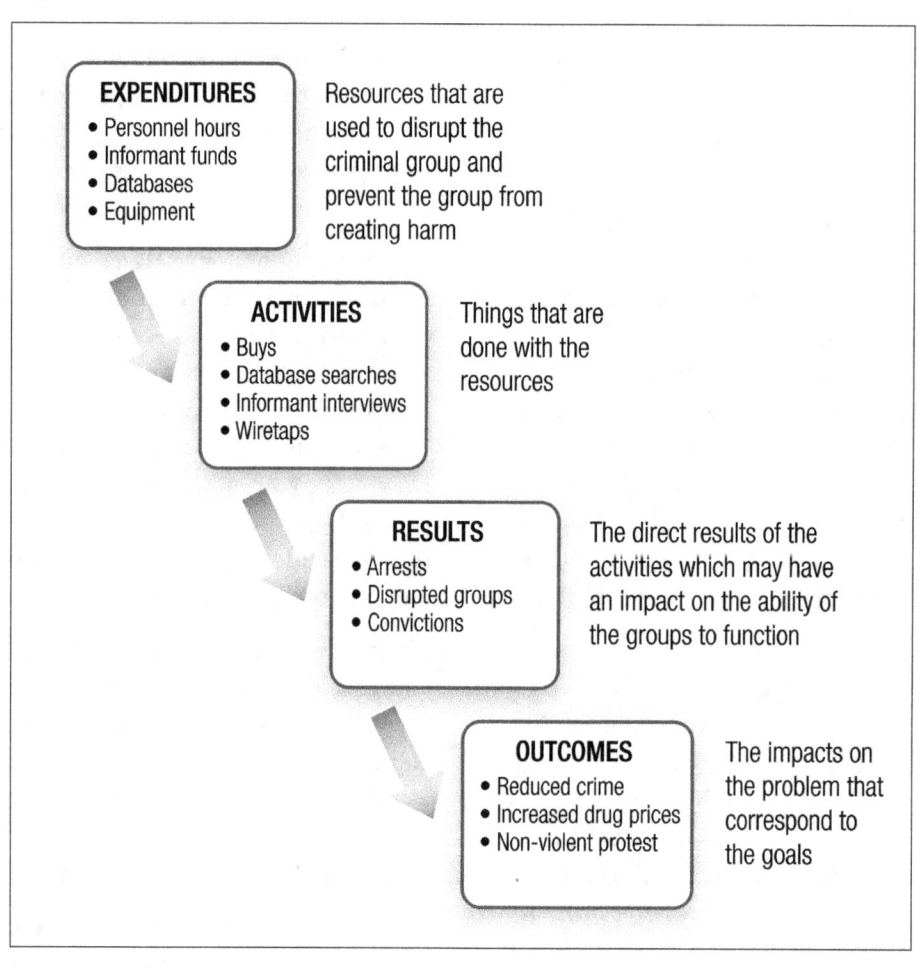

IT IS EASY TO DECEIVE YOURSELF, BUT THIS CAN BE DANGEROUS IN INTELLIGENCE ANALYSIS. When self-deceptions are due to thinking mistakes they are called *cognitive traps;* when due to how the intelligence function is organized, they are called *groupthink.*

Cognitive traps

Richard Heuer shows how intelligence failures result from three limitations of our thinking:

1. When our minds have too much information to process they discard data they judge to be irrelevant.

2. When facts are missing or the quality of data is in doubt, our minds often fill in gaps.

3. When there is limited time available to assess the data, our minds jump to conclusions.

These limitations result in our minds using short cuts, or **heuristics**, to speed up thinking. Heuristics are helpful in everyday situations when they fit the situation, and when the costs of being wrong are small. **Cognitive traps** arise when the heuristics do not fit the situation.

Table 16 on page 78 and 79 lists common heuristics and related cognitive traps in the first three columns. The fourth column describes situations where the heuristics can be useful. The last column describes ways of avoiding traps when the heuristic does not apply.

Groupthink

Groupthink is the tendency of a team to reach a conclusion that reduces internal conflict, rather than addresses the problem. It is most prevalent when the team: (a) lacks diversity; (b) is isolated from groups that may have alternative points of view; and (c) has no clear rules for decision making that make it safe to voice conflicting opinions. Groupthink becomes worse when the team's decision making is dominated by a single person or faction. In the extreme, a senior police executive or elected official dictates a party line that constrains the team's analysis.

Groupthink can be reduced; (a) by increasing the diversity of backgrounds and experience of participants; (b) by creating explicit rules for

discussion that require airing opposing viewpoints; and (c) by promoting values of getting the story right and reducing the problem, rather than creating a consensus and focusing on enforcement.

Judge the strength and weight of evidence. *Strength refers to the role the evidence plays in confirming or falsifying a hypothesis. Weight refers to the degree that the evidence can be trusted.* An informant may report that leaders from two rival gangs recently met to plan an attack on a third gang. This confirms analysis about the changing relationships among gangs. If the informant has a history of spreading false rumors or it is doubtful that the informant could have firsthand knowledge of the meeting, then the weight of the evidence is small, though the strength may be high.

Guard against inflating a problem

Christopher Bruce has reminded us that police and analysts tend to equate their own self-worth with the seriousness of the crimes and the danger posed by the criminal groups they are investigating. Consequently, officers, analysts, and, on occasion, entire police agencies exaggerate certain crime problems. This is largely unintentional, though it might play well in the media and might help garner more resources for the department. However, it can have more pernicious effects. Relatively harmless groups of kids may get treated like gangs, immigrant communities harboring nothing more serious than a few illegal immigrants may be treated like havens of terrorism, and every gathering of motorcycle enthusiasts is policed as if the Hell's Angels are mobilizing for war.

Table 16. Heuristics and cognitive traps in intelligence analysis

HEURISTIC	EXPLANATION	EXAMPLE	WORKS IF...	COUNTERMEASURES
Anchoring	The initial guess strongly influences the final estimate.	An initial estimate that a biker gang has 100 members influences later estimates. If this first guess is wrong, so will be later estimates.	The people making the first estimate have a good track record for accuracy.	Consider multiple first guesses that are very different.
Tunnel vision	Focus on a narrow range of alternatives, often just one.	Only enforcement is considered for addressing an offender group. Other tactics might work better.	There is strong evidence supporting the narrow range of alternatives.	Use evidence-based approaches, when available. When not, seek out a range of alternatives, including unusual ones.
Select the first	Choose the first alternative as being good enough.	The first explanation of the group's behavior that fits the data is chosen. Alternative explanations that might also fit are not considered.	The cost of a mistake is small and speed of decision is critical.	Even when a good explanation is available, brainstorm plausible alternatives that might fit the facts.
Availability	Decisions are based on what comes to mind most easily	Following media reports of a notorious group, analysts label their group as similar.	Prominence of an idea is linked to its validity.	Use brainstorming or other techniques that expand ideas. (See "Select the first.")
Framing	The answer is strongly influenced by how the question is asked.	"How will we break up the group?" points to enforcement; "How will we reduce the harms this group creates?" suggests a wider range of tactics.	The way of asking the question has a track record of leading to success.	Make sure the decision-making group is diverse in background and experience. Invite in outsiders who might ask different questions

Make hypotheses explicit. The more explicit your team is about its assumptions, the more likely it can test its assumptions and avoid costly mistakes. Searching for alternative hypotheses helps reveal hidden assumptions (Step 21). It is much easier to find hidden assumptions when the group places two or more explanations in fair competition and the team engages in systematic searches for data that can falsify one or more of the explanations.

Debrief. Whether the intelligence operation was successful or not, and particularly when it was not, analysts and others involved should systematically go over the experience to document lessons learned.

READ MORE:

Richard Heuer. 2007. *Psychology of Intelligence Analysis.* Hauppauge, New York: Novinka Books.

Kim Rossmo. 2009. *Criminal Investigative Failures.* Boca Raton, Florida: CRC Books.

HEURISTIC	EXPLANATION	EXAMPLE	WORKS IF...	COUNTERMEASURES
Representa-tiveness	Base a judgment on another group that shares some characteristics.	Both groups dealing drugs leads to the conclusion that meth sellers operate like crack dealers.	The characteristic is important and genuinely diagnostic of the problem.	Keep in mind variation. Look for differences as well as similarities.
Identity	Big events must have big causes.	A multiple shooting suggests a planned attack by several shooters, when in fact one shooter acted impulsively when threatened.	The only causes possible are big.	Consider that small, perhaps seemingly inconsequential things, initiated the causal chain.
Correlation	Two events that occur close in time and space must be related.	Analysts conclude that two shootings in one neighborhood in one week are due to gang disputes.	The association has been established by research and it is strong.	Coincidence and randomness are always possible. Look for other evidence beside association.
Confirmation	Look only for evidence that supports a hypothesis.	Having decided that all members of a group come from one neighborhood, only evidence supporting this conclusion is examined.	Evidence in support contradicts all the alternative hypotheses.	Look for contradictory evidence. Consider evidence supporting alternative hypotheses (Step 21).

Adapted from: Rossmo 2009

29

THE PUBLIC ARE OFTEN SKEPTICAL OF CLAIMS FOR THE UTILITY OF INTELLIGENCE ANALYSIS AND CONCERNED ABOUT threats it may pose to personal liberty and democratic values. Others in the police and public feel that it is useful, essential, and poses little threat to democracies or liberty. Examples can be found to support both sets of views. In short, police intelligence is controversial and the controversy will not be resolved any time soon.

Despite this, there can be consensus around specific issues. Most people would agree that certain police intelligence operations are useful and promote democratic values. Excellent examples of this are the directed deterrence projects, based on "Pulling Levers" (Step 26), that have been used across the United States to combat street group-related homicides and street drug dealing. These projects focus police attention on high-violence individuals and groups, and high-volume drug markets. Police implement these projects in collaboration with community groups, and can field them without threatening civil liberties. Focusing reduces the number of individuals brought under police scrutiny and community collaboration provides some transparency. And, it reduces crime.

Protecting individual liberties and constitutional principles is fundamental to policing. There is no debate over this. Because this is so important, it bears repeating, largely because there have been failures in the past to adhere to these standards. Such failures are not simply the fault of individuals; they are the failings of the agencies that employ the individuals. Agencies that rely heavily on law enforcement (and overlook alternatives), employ broad sweeping campaigns (instead of focusing on the most harmful people and places), and measure activities (rather than outcomes) facilitate such failures.

An important way to ensure that intelligence analysis lives up to high ethical standards is to focus on harmful target groups and measure success by outcomes. When success is measured by arrests, seizures, disrupted criminal organizations, and other means, then there is an incentive to produce arrests and seizures, and to announce that criminal groups have been fractured (whether they have been or not).

Shifting the focus to outcomes makes it easier to take the more principled path, but it does not guarantee ethical behavior. When we call for a focus on goals and outcomes we are not claiming that "the ends justify the means." But by stating that there are many means to select among, we are claiming that in most, if not all, circumstances there will be good means that can help achieve the ends desired; it is not a choice between effective bad means, and ineffective good means.

There are 10 principles that if followed will help assure ethical results. Except for the first, they are in no particular order. Indeed, they overlap and are mutually supporting.

1. **Reinforce democratic values.** Open discussion and debate is the foundation of democracy. Many of the principles that follow have their foundation in this principle. Conduct intelligence analysis in a manner that facilitates open discussion and debate. However, know that you cannot divulge all data. In fact, divulging some data will undermine democratic values. Still, to the extent possible, be open about information. Look for ways that allow for open discussion with the public that do not compromise individual liberties, sources of data, or methods for obtaining data. At the very minimum, do not use your position to undermine democratic institutions and processes.

2. **Tell the truth.** Better to say nothing than to give false reports. Though deceiving offenders can produce short-term gains, in the long term they learn about the deceptions. Importantly, the public is also likely to be deceived. In either case, gaining future cooperation from the public or from offenders becomes more difficult.

3. **Tell as much as possible.** You might not be able to tell all, but it is possible to tell much. You do not have to tell it all at one time; some information can be kept secret for a time. Definitely convey the uncertainty in the information shared with the public.

4. **Focus on behaviors, not characteristics.** As much of your intelligence is uncertain, protecting the anonymity of individuals is important. Focus on the behavior of groups, not the characteristics of their members. Do not generalize beyond the specific offenders in question. Do not hold individuals up for public ridicule.

5. **Demonstrate progress.** Focus on the harms done by groups and measure your progress by the reduction in these harms, not by your activities. Focusing on progress toward achieving goals reduces the need to discuss sources, methods, and other things that should be kept confidential. When you describe actions and activities, link them directly to goals and outcomes. Admit setbacks and explain them.

6. **Be truthful to yourself.** Conduct self-assessments of your work. When successful, discover why it worked and how it can be repeated. Acknowledge that some successes were due to good fortune, and may not be repeatable. When unsuccessful, find out why you did not succeed and what you can do to avoid repeats. Identify unforeseen circumstances that impeded success and determine how these can be addressed in the future.

7. **Recognize limits.** Acknowledge that when it comes to crime, all data is suspect, and this is even more the case when dealing with offender groups. Understand that as much as you think you know about a group, or your effect on the group, you probably do not know enough. Appreciate the limits of human cognition and develop ways to reduce their negative impact. Recognize that you are likely to be wrong and that humility is a requirement.

8. **Focus.** Police resources are scarce and the public is most concerned about broad use of police powers. For both reasons, target groups that produce the most harm. Use criminal justice sanctions precisely, and convey credible deterrent threats to group members. When seeking to address locations that facilitate group crimes, pick the exact places that aid the groups, rather than larger areas. Focusing not only expends fewer resources and poses less of a threat to civil liberties, but it is also the most effective approach.

9. **Be wary of false consensus.** The uncertainty inherent in understanding group criminal behavior means that it is highly unlikely that any group of police agents has a full understanding of what is going on. There will always be surprises. Consequently, it is important to create an environment that encourages new ideas, innovative ways of doing things, alternative view points, and dissenting opinions.

10. **Test ideas.** Hypothesis testing is seldom viewed as a moral imperative, but when the truth is uncertain and the stakes are high, it is critical that ideas be put to strong tests. A strong test seeks out information that could falsify the idea. Testing is quintessentially democratic, because it does not rely on the status of the person with the idea, or how many followers that idea has. The idea must survive assault by facts and logic.

30

WE HAVE REPEATEDLY ARGUED IN THIS MANUAL THAT ARRESTING GROUP MEMBERS IS RARELY ENOUGH to solve a crime problem and, in line with the principles of problem-oriented policing, you should work to change the conditions that make the group's crimes possible. However, we are not blind to the difficulties of doing this. Arresting offenders is seen as the prime duty of the police, and a clear legal and procedural framework exists to guide you. On the other hand, changing the facilitating conditions for crime is a much less familiar role for police and you can expect it to be resisted. Furthermore, compared with traditional policing, which has been around since the London Metropolitan Police was founded in 1829, experience in the use of problem-oriented policing is comparatively recent and you can expect its procedures to be less well-defined, if not outright murky.

Our manual has been written to help you, but you can expect to run into roadblocks of two kinds that can delay and discourage you. These are: (1) objections to the idea of reducing opportunities for offenders, and (2) difficulties of changing critical facilitating conditions.

Objections

The source of many objections you might encounter is **the fundamental attribution error**. Psychologists use this term to describe the human tendency to ignore the role of situation and environment in causing behavior. For psychologists, behavior results from the interaction between the organism and the environment. Translated for police, this means that crime results from the interaction of a motivated offender with a crime opportunity. Traditional policing focusses on "taking out" the offender from the equation, while problem-oriented policing seeks also to remove the opportunities for crime. The difficulty is that the public have little understanding that opportunities play a large part in causing crime. They think that crime is solely the result of immorality, selfishness, and greed. As a consequence, you will likely encounter many objections and even accusations as you seek to change the facilitating conditions for the problem you are addressing, such as these below:

1. **You are not doing your job.** That is to say, you are not arresting offenders and bringing them to justice. This argument may be made when you are trying to persuade some individuals—for example shopkeepers, apartment complex managers, owners of pubs and clubs—to change their premises or practices to make crime less likely to occur.

2. **You are blaming the victim and inconveniencing the law-abiding.** Those who accuse you of not doing your job might also claim that you are blaming them for the crime problem, and inconveniencing them with burdensome requirements, when all they are trying to do is run a successful business that provides a service to the public.

3. **You are ignoring displacement.** People tend to believe that offenders will always find a way to commit crime whatever the impediments thrown up against them. It is not only the public that believes this—many police do as well. But there is now ample evidence from research that displacement is a much less common result of reducing opportunities for crime than usually believed. You should be ready to counter the displacement argument by becoming familiar with *Analyzing Crime Displacement and Diffusion*, Problem-Solving Tool Guide No. 10.

Facilitating conditions may be too difficult to change

You can usually deal with the objections listed above through patient explanation (another skill required of those engaged in problem-oriented policing). However, your efforts to change facilitating conditions might run into a more intractable roadblock—some of these conditions just cannot be changed. We are not referring here to obvious facts of geography, such as the proximity to the Mexico border that facilitates theft of cars for export. Instead, we are referring to the limits of local police to persuade key stakeholders to make changes. We identify three sources of these limits below, together with illustrative examples:

1. **Action is needed at regional or national levels.** For example, a facilitator of most varieties of car theft—whether joyriding, theft for resale, or theft for export overseas—is the lack of in-built vehicle security. Only in recent years has effective security, such as electronic ignition immobilizers and central door and window locking, been built-in at manufacture. But the vehicle fleet in the United States now averages more than 10 years in age and, assuming your jurisdiction is typical, most of the cars it encompasses provide easy pickings for thieves. In the long-run, this situation will change as manufacturers increasingly adopt more built-in security, perhaps in response to federal regulation or to meet public demand. Meanwhile, your hands are tied.

2. **Stakeholders may be unable or unwilling to act.** It might be thought that the best way to reduce theft for export to Mexico would be to tighten vehicle inspection at the border. Leaving aside that many stolen cars cross the border before they have been reported stolen, there are several reasons why this is difficult to achieve. First, border security is more heavily focused on incoming than outgoing traffic. Second, number plate recognition devices are prone to malfunction, so their warnings are often ignored. Third, increasing inspection times by just a minute or two will rapidly result in lengthy queues and unacceptable delays. Finally, organized thieves are well-practiced in deceiving hurried inspection procedures. Consequently, what seems to be an obvious and effective way to deal with the problem cannot be implemented.

3. **Changes are too expensive or too disruptive of business models.** Research has clearly shown that two clerks on duty in convenience stores, particularly at slow times, substantially reduce the risks of robbery. Nevertheless, legislation mandating this measure was strenuously resisted in Florida and elsewhere, on grounds that it was too costly. In fact, all businesses, from corner stores to national banks, always compare the costs

of crime prevention with the costs of crimes that might be prevented. When the risks of crime are low, the businesses often prefer to run these risks and call in the police when a crime occurs. They may also resist a crime prevention measure when it requires them to make difficult changes in their usual operations. For example, new home builders in Charlotte resisted police advice, based on solid research, that site burglaries could be reduced if appliances were installed in new homes immediately before the purchasers took up residence rather than weeks before. This was because builders found it was administratively easier to arrange for appliances for a particular housing development to be delivered together and installed all that same time instead of arranging for them to be installed just before each house was occupied.

It may be problems such as these that undermine your problem-oriented policing project. But you should always remember there is never just one way to solve a problem. If you run into a roadblock, turn your attention to another key facilitating condition that you might be able to change. Who knows, you might therefore enjoy the considerable satisfaction of bringing about a lasting reduction in crime.

READ MORE:
Ronald V. Clarke and Herman Goldstein. 2002. "Reducing Theft at Construction Sites." In *Analysis for Crime Prevention.* Vol. 13 of *Crime Prevention Studies.* Monsey, New York: Criminal Justice Press.

Part 2

Case Studies of Criminal Groups and Problem Gatherings

31

IN WRITING THIS MANUAL, WE DISCOVERED THAT WHEREAS CRIME ANALYSIS COVERS THE GENERALITY OF CRIME, intelligence analysis is mostly focused on offending by groups. We had not seen this point made before, but it soon arose in our discussions about intelligence analysis with police analysts—in fact, they mostly took the point for granted.

At first, we treated this idea as a hypothesis, but we gradually became more confident that it does indeed represent the reality of intelligence analysis, at least in the policing field. Consequently, we thought it important to test the idea by undertaking a closer study of a variety of groups and gatherings in order to learn more about:

1. The kinds of information needed to understand them sufficiently well to identify possible points of intervention for problem-oriented policing

2. The guidance provided by the literature about ways to analyze the information that might exist

3. The existing information on the range of measures that have been deployed by police and others to prevent the crimes committed, to apprehend the offenders, and generally to reduce the harms resulting from the actions of the groups and the activities associated with the gatherings

For these purposes, we did not have to cover every kind of criminal organization and problem gathering; indeed, it would have been impossible to do so in the limits of time and pages available. Rather, we sought to include a variety of groups and gatherings, some familiar (e.g., street gangs, retail drug dealers, and street racing) and some less so (Internet pedophile rings, organized insurance fraudsters, and animal rights extremists). In making our selections, we chose not to include groups and gatherings for which published information was sparse. The first eleven case studies describe a wide variety of crime groups and the final five case studies describe a diverse selection of problem gatherings.

While our original objective in assembling this information was to test the ideas we present in the body of the manual, we thought it could be helpful to present summaries of the assembled information in the form of the case studies. If you happen to be dealing with any of the groups or gatherings included here, you might find the relevant case studies to be of direct value in your own intelligence work. More generally useful to you, however, might be the examples they provide of the kinds of intelligence that could be collected for other groups and gatherings, and the kinds of preventive interventions that might be considered. This would be the main benefit of looking through all the case studies once you have finished reading the body of the text.

The goal of these case studies is to provide a general way of approaching criminal groups, rather than provide an encyclopedia of what is known and unknown. This can change rather swiftly, and there is some debate over a number of issues. At the end of each case, we provide a few readings. These are the sources we found most useful. We choose not to provide detailed citations to all the things written on each group. If you find yourself directly addressing one of the types of groups in these case studies, you should do additional research to come up with useful approaches. *Researching a Problem*, one of the Guides from the Center for Problem-Oriented Policing, could help you get started.

The case studies were mostly written by our colleague, Gohar Petrossian. They follow a reasonably standard format adjusted somewhat to the topic and to the available information. They begin with a general overview of the problem, followed by the discussion of the facilitating conditions or factors promoting the problem. Some case studies include sections explaining how these groups are organized. Examples of domestic or international response strategies are presented either in the body of the text or in separate boxes. Lastly, suggestions as to what you might contribute as an intelligence analyst and what your agency can do are provided at the end of each case study. Be aware that these examples are not intended to be exhaustive and, unfortunately, few have been rigorously evaluated. They are included merely to help you and your agency get started!

READ MORE:

Ronald Clarke and Phyllis Schultze. 2004. *Researching a Problem*. Problem-Oriented Guides for Police. Problem-Solving Tool Series No. 2. Washington, D.C.: U.S. Department of Justice, Office of Community Oriented Policing Services.

32

MANY, PERHAPS MOST, POLICE IN THE UNITED STATES HAVE GROUPS OF DRUG DEALERS OPERATING ILLICITLY in their city. The variety of drugs sold makes it difficult to describe the role of intelligence in addressing local drug markets, and we will stick to some broad principles that must be adapted to your local conditions.

Forms of retail drug dealing

Drug markets are where the supply of drugs meets the demand for drugs. They are of two general types:

- **Closed markets.** These operate through social networks. To buy drugs you must know a seller in the network who trusts you, or you need someone who knows a seller. The advantage to all participants is that closed markets offer security from the police, and from robbery by other offenders. For buyers, they can also provide some assurance of product quality because information circulates among the insiders who routinely interact with each other.

- **Open markets.** Participants in these markets may not know each other. Street markets tend to be geographically fixed so that customers can find them. For sellers, the advantage is that they can get more customers, but there are major risks from police and from robbery. Open markets tend to be more violent than closed markets because they are less secure. Open markets can become convergent settings (Step 12) and thereby foster criminal activity in their surroundings.

Open markets are a much more serious problem for communities than are closed markets: not only are they more violent, but they cater to larger numbers of people and they are more visible to the public.

What are the facilitating conditions?

- **Consumers.** A relatively few high-volume consumers and many small-time users are needed.

- **Supply.** The dealer must be connected with people who can supply drugs. Suppliers are often organized in a "cottage industry" style where small groups form and disband as necessary. They may travel from small cities to larger metropolitan areas to secure drugs to supply their local dealers. Such suppliers are easily replaced.

- **Financing.** There are two ways drug dealing can be financed:

  1. The dealer uses his own money to purchase drugs. The supplier gets paid up front and the dealer pockets the proceeds from the sales. Small-scale operations can function this way.

  2. The supplier provides the drugs on credit, and the dealer pays him back from the proceeds. This requires either trust or an enforcement mechanism. This increases the risks of violence.

Though these are the dominant financing arrangements, others are possible. For example, a dealer might provide enforcement services to a supplier in exchange for drugs, or pay for drugs with stolen goods or firearms.

- **Social networks of buyers and sellers.** For closed markets the minimal requirement is a social network of individuals, some of whom want drugs and others who have drugs to sell. This may be the dominant form of drug sales as it has the fewest requirements.

- **Neighborhoods.** Open drug markets require locations that are easily accessible to customers and where their operations will not be disrupted by property owners. Low-income neighborhoods are ideal locations because much of the property is owned by absentee landlords who have little incentive to intervene because of the low economic return on their properties. Once established, drug sellers tend to congregate near each other, just like legitimate businesses, if the area suitable for drug dealing is big enough to accommodate them without conflict.

■ **Streets.** Large open markets need ready access to customers. So these tend to be on or near major arterial routes or highways, within vulnerable neighborhoods. Street patterns that permit circular cruising give customers the ability to locate dealers quickly and leave.

■ **Places.** These are open markets where people can legitimately hang out and where owners will not interfere. Corner convenience stores are useful because dealers and customers can blend in. Nearby rental apartments where landlords are not scrupulous about tenant management provide locations for stashing drugs, meeting suppliers, and resting places. Lax place management is critical in all circumstances.

What is being done?

There has been a shift in attention from policing drug networks to policing drug places. The rise of hot spots policing has led to intensive patrolling of small areas with high crime concentrations. If these concentrations are close to drug markets, the markets suffer from these patrols. Problem-oriented approaches have been found to be effective in suppressing open drug markets, and superior to hot spots policing alone. Most successful problem solving has engaged the owners of properties—landlords, retailers, bar owners, and so forth—in making their locations unsuitable for dealing. Typically, these place managers cooperate. But when they do not, public pressure and the threat of civil sanctions can be helpful. Many landlords are woefully ignorant about crime and drug dealing, so landlord training can be helpful.

Street closures and other traffic manipulations can also be helpful in specific circumstances. When dealers and users take advantage of easy access to market sites, then altering traffic flow by changing street access can be helpful.

What can you do?

Differentiate between open and closed markets, but recognize that some markets may use aspects of each.

Keep a current list of open and closed markets in your area.

Rank markets by the three Vs:

■ Violence—killings, shootings, and assaults

■ Volume—number of dealers, sellers, and transactions

■ Visibility—how noticeable to the public

Determine how dealers in the most problematic markets either finance their supplies or get protection for their operations.

Know who the dealers are and who they associate with.

For open markets you could identify places critical for market operation and their owners/managers; study street patterns that allow buyers to meet sellers; or identify facilitating conditions that can be altered at the place, street, and in the immediate area.

For closed markets you could gather intelligence on how these develop and interact; and identify those which are most problematic using the three Vs—violence, volume, visibility.

What can your agency do?

Set priorities. Put high-violence markets (usually open markets) at the top of the list for closing down.

Drive illicit drug use underground. Drug dealing cannot be eliminated, but it can be reduced. Displacing open markets to closed can reduce each of the three Vs: violence, volume, and visibility.

Engage place owners. Involve owners and managers of locations at risk of drug dealing. This will include apartment owners and managers, bar owners and employees, entertainment venue owners and employees, and others.

Address street patterns and traffic flow. Alter street patterns that assist open drug dealing. Gain the active participation of local residents and businesses to minimize collateral damage to legitimate activities.

Communicate directly with the dealers. Creating a credible direct deterrent threat to dealers has been shown to reduce open drug dealing. This approach operates very much like "pulling levers" (Step 26).

READ MORE:

Alex Harocopos and Mike Hough. 2005. *Drug Dealing in Open-Air Markets.* Problem-Oriented Guides for Police. Problem-Specific Guides Series, No. 31. Washington, D.C.: U.S. Department of Justice, Office of Community Oriented Policing Services.

Rana Sampson. 2001. *Drug Dealing in Privately Owned Apartment Complexes.* Problem-Oriented Guides for Police. Problem-Specific Guides Series, No. 4. Washington, D.C.: U.S. Department of Justice, Office of Community Oriented Policing Services.

Ronald V. Clarke. 2005. *Closing Streets and Alleys to Reduce Crime: Should You Go Down This Road?* Problem-Oriented Guides for Police. Response Guides Series, No. 2. Washington, D.C.: U.S. Department of Justice, Office of Community Oriented Policing Services.

33 TERRORISTS

UNTIL 2001, YOUR CHIEF MIGHT RARELY HAVE THOUGHT ABOUT THE THREAT OF TERRORISM, but 9/11 changed that. However remote the threat of an attack may be, the consequences can be so horrific that police must now spend precious resources on prevention and preparation.

Apart from being an act of unparalleled evil, 9/11 was unusual because its perpetrators were foreign terrorists. This might have signaled an increase in foreign attacks, though until then the great majority of attacks had been perpetrated by domestic terrorists, such as eco-terrorists, anti-abortionists, hate groups, and militias. The most lethal attack by domestic terrorists was the 1995 car bombing of the federal building in Oklahoma by Timothy McVeigh.

Domestic terrorists have not been able to conduct repeated attacks, with the relatively minor exceptions in the 1960s of the black power movement, and the bombings carried out by the Puerto Rican Liberation movements in the 1960s and 1970s. Could repeated terrorist attacks again happen here? These are some possible sources of risk:

- A long history of violence among Latino and other gangs in large U.S. cities, some of whom are composed of former paramilitary extremists such as the Mara Salvatrucha deriving from El Salvador.

- Deportation of illegal immigrant gang members back to their home country, thus creating the opportunities to establish international networks.

- Existence of well-established immigrant communities that provide cultural cover for potential terrorists.

What can your department do to avert an attack?

The most important things to do are to strengthen community policing, particularly of immigrant communities, and develop links with fusion centers and the FBI Joint Terrorism Task Force.

What can you do, as an intelligence analyst, to support your chief? You should:

- Learn about terrorism so that you know what kind of intelligence to assemble. Start with *Policing Terrorism*, listed in "Read more." (Since terrorism myths abound, *Myths about terrorism* on page 92 includes those discussed in *Policing Terrorism*.)

- While accepting that the risk of attack for most cities is very low, try to determine which factors could increase the risk for your city (see Brief 8 in *Policing Terrorism*).

- Develop local intelligence by analyzing reports from police officers, particularly community officers in areas where potential terrorists might feel comfortable, and from businesses such as motels, banks, and car rental agencies (see Step 16). The San Diego Police Department routinely monitors reports of the theft of propane canisters from suppliers and e-mails the information to its investigators and analysts.

- Identify possible targets for attack in your jurisdiction. Begin by drawing up three lists:

  1. A short list of the most obvious targets to be protected as soon as possible. (For guidance, see Briefs 29 and 30 of *Policing Terrorism*.)

  2. A prioritized list of other targets that require extensive target hardening and a timetable for ensuring that this is done.

  3. A longer list of all possible targets that should be protected by some basic target hardening measures that your department should work to get put in place.

READ MORE:

Graeme Newman and Ronald Clarke. 2008. *Policing Terrorism: An Executive's Guide.* Washington D.C.: U.S. Department of Justice, Office of Community Oriented Policing Services.

Myths about terrorism

1. *Anyone might be a terrorist.* A white-haired grandmother from the Midwest, even if behaving suspiciously, is very unlikely to be a terrorist. More likely is that she is confused or ignorant of the rules, and that should be the assumption when police approach her. They should reserve their suspicions for those who most closely fit the terrorist profile.

2. *Every immigrant is suspect.* Those who fit the terrorist profile best (for the present at least) are young male immigrants of Arab appearance. Among this group, only a tiny minority are wannabe terrorists or even terrorist sympathizers. Assume in your dealings with immigrant groups that they are as opposed to terrorism as anyone else.

3. *Terrorists are crazed fanatics.* However much we disagree with their reasoning and condemn their cruelty, cold rationality guides much of their behavior. Like all organized criminals, they carefully plan their acts, they try to avoid being caught, and they are determined to succeed.

4. *Terrorists are eager to die.* As we know, some terrorists are willing to die for their cause, but many are careful with their lives. They have the same ambitions for success and happiness as everyone else, and they would prefer to escape and strike again rather than fail and die.

5. *Terrorists are evil geniuses.* Not every terrorist has the mind attributed to Osama bin Laden. Most are ordinary, fallible individuals. They might carefully plan their acts, but they cannot anticipate every eventuality and they will be forced to improvise and take chances. This will sometimes result in failure and perhaps in being killed.

6. *Terrorists might strike anywhere.* Only in theory they might; in practice they must conserve their resources and strike for the greatest effect. If we think like terrorists we can anticipate their choices and act accordingly to protect the most vulnerable targets.

7. *Terrorists are unstoppable.* Most groups of terrorists last only one or two years before falling apart. There are also many examples of terrorism being substantially reduced. For example, the Israelis have reduced suicide bombings by installing border fences.

8. *We can win the war on terrorism.* We can hinder the terrorists and make them less successful, but we can never eliminate terrorism from our world. That is about as unlikely as winning the war on crime.

9. *If it can happen in London (Israel, Delhi…), it can happen here.* Do not assume that a form of terrorism that occurs overseas can easily be reproduced here. Each form of terrorism depends crucially on the opportunities provided by the environment in which it is committed. This environment is rarely the same from country to country. For example, the routine suicide bombings that used to be committed in Israel were made possible by the close proximity of Palestine, the relative ease of entering Israel, and the steady supply of willing bombers. Such conditions do not exist here.

10. *We must prepare for nuclear attack.* Most experts agree that the logistics of building or stealing, and delivering a nuclear bomb make it unlikely terrorists would attack us in this way. Planting a "suitcase bomb" (a radiological dispersal device) in any of our large cities would be much easier. That this would lead to mass casualties is unlikely, though it might result in widespread panic.

11. *Fighting terrorism is a job for the feds.* The FBI and the CIA cannot defeat terrorism on their own. They must garner the support of the public, the private sector, and above all, police agencies. Local police have a key role in gathering intelligence about terrorists, in helping to protect vulnerable targets, and in responding to any attack.

12. *Sharing intelligence is the key to defeating terrorism.* However much we improve intelligence we could never rely on it alone. We also need systematically to reduce the opportunities for terrorism by protecting the most vulnerable targets. Local police might be excused for failing to unearth a terror plot; but there is no excuse for failing to protect key targets or fumbling the response in the event of an attack.

34 WHITE SUPREMACISTS

MEMBERS OF WHITE SUPREMACIST GROUPS BELIEVE THAT WHITES SHOULD DOMINATE SOCIETY because they are superior to other races. They hold in contempt not only other races, ethnicities, and non-protestant religions, but also gays and lesbians. Sometimes they commit hate crimes against these groups. They share a common ideological focus to clean up "cultural pollution" in the United States.

Group members tend to be middle-aged males, average in terms of income, occupation, and level of education. Since 9/11, some white supremacist groups have actively sought to recruit current and former members of the U.S. Armed Services in order to exploit their access to restricted areas and intelligence, or to apply their specialized training in weapons, tactics, and organizational skills.

More than 500 white supremacist groups are thought to exist in the United States, with an overall membership of 100,000 to 200,000. They publish more than 50 periodicals and have established about 2,000 different hate sites on the Internet. They now increasingly rely on the Internet to express their views, recruit new members, and sell their products. Five main groups of white supremacists are as follows:

1. **The Identity Church** incorporates some of the most active and violent organizations, including "Aryan Nations," "Covenant and Sword," and "Arm of the Lord." They seek to justify their racist and anti-Semitic beliefs in a scriptural reading that posits white Christians as God's "chosen" people. They see Jews, defined as non-white, as the greatest enemy, whose ultimate plan is to "race mix" the white race out of existence by brainwashing white women into the arms of black men. On the other hand, they view Blacks as "pre-adamic," a race incapable of creativity and intellectual labor and of constructing a "civilization" or "culture." Followers of the Identity Church ideology believe in the inevitability of a global war between races, which they see as the only way to create a white homeland.

2. **Neo-Nazis** such as the "National Socialist White People's Party" and the "National Alliance," use tracts of Germany's Third Reich to inform their "Americanism" and "White-power" rhetoric.

3. **Skinheads** share neo-Nazi rhetoric and ideology in a somewhat less orderly and consistent manner. According to the Anti-Defamation League (www. adl.org), their numbers may be increasing. They tend to be younger, more loosely organized, but also more violent than some other hate groups.

4. The **Ku Klux Klan**, though once powerful and prominent, is currently in a state of fragmentation. In its contemporary form, it addresses problems like AIDS, crime, welfare, or immigration "solely through the prism of race and offers not solutions but a license to hate." (June A. Marlin. 1992. *Klan's Invisible Empire is Alive and Active in Northeast.* Available at http://alb.merlinone.net/mweb/wmsql.wm.request?oneimage&imageid=5618828.)

5. The *Posse Comitatus* (Latin for 'power of the county') shares the anti-Semitism of other hate groups, alongside the anti-statism of the militia groups. The only legitimate form of government for the Posse Comitatus exists at the local level, since the federal government is dominated by Jewish financial interests.

Conditions that promote the emergence of white supremacist groups or facilitate their actions

Such conditions include the following:

- Uncertain economic times, farm crises, and perceived threats to rural industries
- Social changes, such as the rise of the women's movement, the civil rights movement, and gay and lesbian movements
- High rates of non-white immigration
- A volatile political atmosphere, such as that surrounding the wars in Iraq and Afghanistan
- The election, in 2008, of America's first African American president

- The existence of radical churches in rural states

- Lax gun controls in these states

- Internet providers that tolerate hate messages on web pages

It is immediately obvious that very little can be done to change these societal conditions, although the House of Representatives passed the Local Law Enforcement Hate Crimes Prevention Act 2007 to provide federal assistance to state and local jurisdictions to prosecute hate crimes. In fact, local and state police are perhaps in the best position to take action against such groups.

What can you do?

Learn about hate groups and identify those active in your area. Gather intelligence about their ideologies and their backgrounds, and identify possible targets of these groups.

Gather intelligence about the leaders of the hate groups. Where legal grounds for arrest exist, removing the leader will significantly impact the functional capability of the group.

Use analysis to identify possible target locations and select areas at risk. Inform your department about possible future attacks.

Identify and monitor websites operated by hate groups active in your jurisdiction.

Study the *modus operandi* in hate crimes. This may help prevent future attacks on similar targets.

What can your agency do?

Form a task force trained to recognize and properly respond to hate crime if and when it occurs in your jurisdiction.

Warn the leaders of organizations targeted by hate groups to watch out for possible signs of hate crimes and encourage them to contact your agency if alarmed.

Encourage the community to report hate crimes and employ its assistance in investigating and responding to hate crime incidents, and in apprehending the perpetrators.

Seek help from state and federal law enforcement if the groups' operational outreach is beyond your jurisdiction and more sophisticated investigative tools are necessary to support your current operations.

Identify and disrupt any gatherings that use racial slogans, anti-Semitic themes, or any other white supremacist ideology to carry out their activities and recruit new members.

Identify and remove (if possible) the possible financial sources of these groups.

Four characteristics of enduring white supremacist groups

1. Strong leaders with a clear ideological agenda as, for example, in the cases of the Aryan Nations and the National Alliance.
2. Consistent pursuit of activities to expand their goals and acquire the necessary finances. Most groups have perpetrated serious crimes on a regular basis, which has contributed to group stability.
3. Strategic advantage taken of political opportunities. The broader political atmosphere feeds these groups with the opportunities to further their ideologies.
4. Internal cohesion. Organizational instability is seen as a major threat to the survival of these groups. This can result from conflict among its leaders, loss/ removal of leadership or the inner core, and the loss of funds.

Source: Freilich, Chermak, and Caspi 2009.

Operation Lone Wolf

In 1998, the San Diego P.D. began to investigate a hate crime case where several prominent members of the community and religious locations were targeted. The two-year investigation resulted in the arrest and prosecution of Alex Curtis, a well-known white supremacist leader. Curtis had been involved for many years in promoting and fostering racial violence through his website, telephone hotlines, and newspaper (*The Nationalist Observer*). He targeted businesses owned and operated by Jewish people, as well as elected officials or known public figures who either openly spoke against white supremacist activities, or who helped minorities. The investigation also led to the arrest of Curtis' cell members. Following the arrests, San Diego experienced a dramatic decrease in hate crimes.

Source: San Diego P.D. 2001. Herman Goldstein Award. Available at www.popcenter.org/library/awards/goldstein/2001/01-60.pdf.

READ MORE:

Neil Chakraborti and Jon Garland. 2009. *Hate Crime: Impact, Causes and Responses.* Thousand Oaks, California: Sage Publications, Ltd.

Joshua D. Freilich, Steven M. Chermak, and David Caspi. 2009. Critical events in the life trajectories of domestic extremist white supremacist groups. *Criminology and Public Policy* 8(3): 497–530.

35

ANIMAL RIGHTS EXTREMISTS, AND MEMBERS OF GROUPS ENGAGED IN THIS KIND OF CRIMINAL ACTIVITY, are generally young to middle-aged, white, and well-educated. Thus, they draw from the same pool of individuals who are attracted to organizations that work peacefully for animal rights, such as Greenpeace, the Wilderness Society, and People for the Ethical Treatment of Animals.

SHAC (Stop Huntingdon Animal Cruelty) is an extremist animal rights group. In 1999, it almost succeeded in shutting down Huntingdon Life Sciences, a British company that conducts product safety testing on animals. SHAC employed a combination of intimidation and violent protests and, since then, extremist groups have become increasingly violent and are said to have caused millions of dollars' worth of damage.

How are they organized?

The best-known animal rights extremist group is the Animal Liberation Front (ALF). It was established in Great Britain in the 1970s as an outgrowth of groups such as Greenpeace and the Sea Shepherd Conservation Society. It consists of an unknown number of individual cells made up of a few people who act autonomously. The activists remain largely anonymous to both the public and each other, which is done purposefully to maximize the security and fluidity of the movement. The ALF operates in more than a dozen countries, including France, New Zealand, Poland, Italy, and Slovakia.

Apart from this group, other lesser-known groups have claimed responsibility for criminal actions in defense of animals. These include the Animal Rights Militia; the Justice Department,[1] a UK-based extremist group; Bakers for Animal Liberation; Guerilla Advertising Contingent; Kangaroo Wilderness Defense; the Lawn Liberation Front; and Pirates for Animal Liberation. The Animal Rights Militia, the Justice Department, and SHAC have been especially active and violent in both the United States and Great Britain in recent years.

What criminal activity are these groups engaged in?

Researchers have classified the criminal activities of these groups into four groups:

- *Type I* commit minor crimes, involving little property damage, which may include such acts as civil disobedience, hanging banners, spray painting slogans, and smashing windows.

- *Type II* commit significant acts of property damage, including setting fire to research laboratories and using firebombs or incendiary devices.

- *Type III* engage in threatening behavior directed against people, including bomb hoaxes, e-mail threats, harassing phone calls, splashing people with red paint, pelting people with tofu pies, leaving dead animals on dinner plates, etc.

- *Type IV* make physical attacks against persons, including beatings and bombings.

Who and what is at risk?

The locations most at risk include federal research facilities, universities, factory farming operations, furriers, and fast-food restaurants. The groups use stolen footage from labs to create publicity materials and films. Research scientists, corporate officials, and their families are at heightened risk of being threatened or assaulted.

The groups use three forms of attack: (a) primary targeting, which can involve visits to the homes of those directly involved in using animals and delivering threats or violence; (b) secondary targeting that involves attacks on companies doing business with animal-related institutions, such as banks; and (c) tertiary targeting that involves harassing the customers or workers of these companies because they are doing business with animal-related institutions.

---

1. The Justice Department is an extreme animal rights group based in the United Kingdom. See: Anti-Defamation League. 2010. "Justice Department Claims Responsibility for Threats Against UCLA Animal Researcher." December 3.

Intelligence Analysis for Problem Solvers

In the 1990s, Operation Bite Back and Operation Bite Back III, multistage campaigns led by the ALF, included the release of more than 10,000 mink from the Arritola Mink Farm in Mt. Angel, Oregon—the largest number of animals released to that time. These and other actions by the ALF led to legislation, including the federal Animal Enterprise Protection Act (1992), which criminalized causing more than $10,000 in damages at commercial and academic institutions that use animals.

Examples of action taken against extremists

The National Association for Biomedical Research (NABR) developed a coalition for research groups and pushed for the passage of the Animal Enterprise Terrorism Act in 2006. The Act is designed to protect enterprises and researchers who are engaged in animal-related research from the forceful, violent, and threatening acts of animal rights extremists. The Act protects not only primary, but also secondary parties, such as suppliers, from harassment, intimidation, threat, and violence.

California has been a prime target for animal activist attacks in the United States and has passed laws to address the problem. In 2008, for example, former Assemblyman Gene Mullin led an effort to pass the Researcher Protection Act, which made it a misdemeanor to publish personal information about researchers or their families, "with the intent that another person imminently uses the information to commit a crime involving violence or a threat of violence against the academic researcher or his or her immediate family member." The Act also outlaws entering the property of academic researchers to intimidate them and to cause them to stop their work.

Cedars-Sinai Medical Center in Los Angeles is one of many institutions that have adopted a variety of security measures. In addition to carefully screening employees before they are hired, these measures include changing the location of the research facility from the ground floor to a higher floor, instituting strict access controls (researchers can only enter the facility by using electronic key cards), and controlling the elevators by using security guards with key-cards for access.

The research community at large has undertaken public outreach to help people understand that animal research is necessary for medical progress and is heavily regulated by the government.

What promotes animal rights extremism?

- The existence of medical, university, or pharmaceutical research facilities that conduct experiments on animals
- Absence of laws protecting researchers and research institutions
- "Factory farming" operations
- Financial support given to these extremist groups by animal lovers

What can you do?

Collect intelligence on the most active groups and members within these groups through their websites and other sources. Determine if any of these groups are active in your jurisdiction or nearby.

Monitor their websites to identify any material used to threaten or frighten their intended victims.

Identify the methods and technology used by these groups to attack their victims.

Determine which type of criminal activity (refer to the four types discussed above) each group is likely to be engaged in (or has historically engaged in) and devise prevention strategies accordingly.

What can your agency do if extremists pose a threat?

Raise awareness about these groups through community meetings and publicity. Inform the public about the methods and technology used by these groups to attack their targets.

Encourage institutions or people most at risk to report any threat, harassment, or intimidation they may experience from animal rights extremist groups.

Inform these potential targets of security measures and responses that they can develop to protect themselves from current or future attacks, intimidation, or harassment.

Advocate legislative changes to control the criminal activities of these groups.

Control or limit any demonstrations that may result in criminal activity by these groups. Coordinate response strategies with other criminal justice agencies or agencies in nearby jurisdictions.

Support any efforts of the local research community to raise awareness about the importance of medical research.

Urge animal lovers not to give money to these extremist groups by informing them about the harms suffered by victims who are attacked.

READ MORE:

Don Liddick. 2006. *Eco-Terrorism: Radical Environmental and Animal Liberation Movements.* Westport, Connecticut: Praeger.

Home Office. 2004. *Animal Welfare-Human Rights: Protecting People from Animal Rights Extremists.* London: Communications Directorate.

PEDOPHILIA IS CLASSIFIED AS A MENTAL DISORDER AND IS DEFINED BY AN INTENSE DESIRE TO ENGAGE IN SEXUAL ACTIVITY with prepubescent children. However, many pedophiles claim that there is nothing abnormal about sexual activity between adults and children. These days, many pedophile rings operate and spread through the Internet. These include Candyman, Shangri-La, Girls 12–16, and Innocent Images, with a combined membership of many thousands.

Pedophile rings engage in a variety of activities, including:

■ **The production and distribution of child pornography,** which is used not only for sexual stimulation and gratification, but also to assist in the seduction of a child, to lower the child's inhibitions, and to show what the offender wants the child to do. This is known as "grooming." Some pedophiles keep pictures of their sexual activity with children. These can be used to either pressure the child to remain silent about the activity, to exchange with other collectors, or to establish bona fides when making contact with other group members.

■ **Distribution of information** about past or present child victims, access routes to vulnerable children, possible victim locations—such as special schools and hostels—methods and tips on grooming, and information on other pedophiles engaged in organized sexual abuse of children. Many different ways exist of distributing these materials, including e-groups, newsgroups, chat rooms, bulletin board systems, e-mail, websites, and peer-to-peer networks. Predators also use Internet social networking sites, such as MySpace, Twitter, and Facebook, to locate minors, and they can also use the Internet to carry out "live" chats with potential victims and to have "virtual sex" with the children.

■ **Support groups** to promote such goals as "sexual liberation for all persons." The most prominent of the U.S. support groups is the North American Man/Boy Love Association (NAMBLA), but others include the Childhood Sensuality Circle, Pedophiliacs Anonymous, and Pedophile Information Exchange. They prepare materials and newsletters advocating legalization of sexual relations between adults and children. They serve to justify pedophilia in the members' minds and reinforce the belief that society, not the pedophile, is misguided.

■ **Financial profit.** In many cases, the websites sell child pornography and can realize substantial profits for the operators. People involved in selling child pornography can be either pedophiles themselves, or people who are not sexually attracted to children but rather are motivated solely by financial gain.

What facilitates Internet child pornography rings?

■ Lack of legal regulation of the Internet

■ Cross-jurisdictional differences in laws and regulations regarding child pornography on the Internet

■ Lack of law enforcement knowledge about the Internet

■ The extensive possibilities the Internet provides to hide the users' identities

■ The international operations of many of the pedophile rings

■ The sophistication and availability of technology (e.g., mobile phones with cameras) that enhances the pedophiles' activities on and off the Internet

■ The volume of Internet daily activity that makes it impossible to track every site and every person visiting these sites

■ The affordability and ease of creating and operating new websites (operators can easily shut down a website that the police are investigating and open a new one)

- Pedophile rings that are knowledgeable about security measures, which can be employed to avoid detection. (Internet sting operations may have succeeded only in catching inexperienced operators)

- The historic reluctance of Internet Service Providers (ISPs) to monitor and censor content

- The reluctance of many victims (and their families) to report abuse

- A widespread perception that child abuse is committed by strangers, not by friends or relations

- The reluctance of parents to monitor their children's computer use

- The existence of pedophile support groups that encourage/justify such activities

Examples of actions taken against Internet child pornography rings

Police sting operations have identified and removed online pedophile rings. For example, Operation PIN, which established a "honeypot" website claiming to offer child pornography, involved the police from Australia, Canada, the U.K., and the United States. As the browsers clicked through screens warning of the explicit nature of the content, they came to a screen that announced that their attempt to obtain online child pornography had been traced and would be reported to local police.

In the United States, ISPs are legally required to report known illegal activity on their sites, but they are not required to search actively for such sites. Police may apply for a court order to seize ISP accounts. Microsoft has announced the development of the Child Exploitation Tracking System that links information, such as credit card purchases, Internet chat room messages, and conviction histories.

Some non-profit organizations seek to raise public awareness about Internet child pornography and will act as political lobby groups. These groups include Wired Safety and Safeguarding Our Children-United Mothers.

The National Center for Missing and Exploited Children operates a CyberTipline that allows parents and children to report child pornography and other incidents of sexual exploitation of children.

What can you do?

Cooperate with your department specialists in Internet crime. They know how to access encrypted sites and e-mails, which may be necessary for gathering intelligence about these groups.

Monitor the activities of child pornography groups, newsgroups, websites, and chat rooms. Postings on these sites for other pedophiles can be used to gather intelligence about online and off-line activities. For example, some sites list member's e-mail addresses to encourage private communication. This information can be used, instead, to gather intelligence and launch an investigation.

What can your agency do?

Authorize officers to enter pedophile newsgroups, chat rooms, or P2P networks posing as pedophiles and request child pornography images from others in the group. They can also enter child or teen groups posing as children and engage pedophiles who may send pornography or suggest a meeting.

In 1996, the San Jose (California) P.D. investigated a complaint against a man who had sexually molested and photographed a 10-year-old girl at a children's party given by his adult daughter in her home. The images were later transmitted via the Internet to members of what turned out to be the Orchid Club. The investigation into that club extended to a number of countries, including the U.K. Examination of the offender's computer uncovered links to the Wonderland Club, another covert pedophile group that used password protection and encryption to hide their activities. The case led to a worldwide investigation of members of both clubs, as well as to the discovery of a third club, the Roundtable.

Source: Associated Press. 1998. "Disgrace follows child porn bust." November 7.

Establish a well-publicized e-mail "hot line," which can be used to report any indications of distribution of child pornography.

Set up a "honey trap site" that purports to contain child pornography, which can be used to capture the IP address or credit card details of visitors trying to download images.

Involve the local community, which can help in raising awareness about the problem, as well as coming forward with information that may assist in arresting and prosecuting perpetrators.

Cooperate with local non-profit organizations in raising awareness about these groups through visits to local schools and youth centers.

READ MORE:

Richard Wortley and Stephen Smallbone. 2006. *Child Pornography on the Internet.* Problem-Oriented Guides for Police. Problem-Specific Guides Series, No. 41. Washington, D.C.: U.S. Department of Justice, Office of Community Oriented Policing Services.

Tony Krone. 2005. *International Police Operations against Online Child Pornography.* Trends and Issues in Crime and Criminal Justice, No. 296. Australian Institute of Criminology.

37

HARDLY ANY AMERICAN CITY IS ENTIRELY FREE OF GRAFFITI, MOST OF WHICH IS GANG-RELATED, HATE-INSPIRED, or simply vandalism. Much less common is "art graffiti," where the motive is to create a startling or even beautiful decoration on a publicly visible surface, such as the side of the building. Since this is done without the owner's consent, the graffiti shows the artist's daring and contempt for the law.

Art graffiti is often committed by organized groups or "crews." Most members are males aged 8–19, most are poor, and they come from a variety of ethnic backgrounds.

Crews choose highly visible sites for their graffiti, such as subway routes, rooftops, freeway walls, billboards, and bridges. They prefer sites that involve some element of risk and that will be seen by other crews. They sometimes choose locations, "walls of fame," near other writers' tags to achieve a symbolic co-presence with them. They might write compliments near well-executed pieces or cross out ("dis") or paint over ("go over") poor works.

To increase their status, graffiti crews may "go citywide" or might "tag the heavens" by writing on tall buildings. They often work at night, which gives them time to cover a greater area. They prefer the cold winter months, because the nights are longer, fewer police and others are about, and overcoats allow spray-cans to be easily concealed.

Graffiti crews sometimes engage in shoplifting, handling stolen goods, marijuana use, and drinking in public. They rarely belong to street gangs, but may be recruited by gangs to develop a tag for gang clothing, to mark the gang's territory, or to paint "Rest in Peace" murals for those who have died on the streets. In return, the taggers gain protection from the gang and are sometimes rewarded with drugs.

A tag is the writer's name or alias, or the name of the crew to which he belongs. Each writer tries to develop a distinctive tag that allows him to "get up" or be recognized by other graffiti artists.

Crews create more complex forms, called "throw-ups" and "pieces" or "murals." Throw-ups are generally multicolored and use large "bubble" or sausage-shaped letters. They may include personal symbols or tiny self-portraits. Pieces or murals are large-scale, multi-colored features that may include human figures, animals, and urban structures.

How are crews organized?

Crews range in size from as few as three to as many as several dozen individuals. They are formed for companionship and for undertaking pieces in difficult to reach locations or that entail risky and time consuming work. While crews have no formal hierarchy, members will take responsibility for certain tasks, depending on their standing in the group. Some work mopping up, filling in the colors, and serving as lookouts, while others write the pieces.

In addition to tagging or "piecing" together, crews may hold regular "art sessions" to work on collective designs, share the "piecebooks" in which they draw their designs, and hone their talents to create future large pieces.

Crews might make contact with other crews by going to "writers' corners," which are locations where they can meet established writers, exchange ideas, and, sometimes go out and hit together. Generally these writers' corners move around as a response to police crackdowns and increased surveillance.

Why become a graffiti artist?

- "Getting up" satisfies a need for recognition and respect. Belonging to a graffiti crew also provides a medium through which artists 'communicate' with each other

- A desire to "escape real life" through creating a new name and establishing a new identity—thus becoming a different person

- The illegal nature of the act provides excitement and re-affirms masculinity

Intelligence Analysis for Problem Solvers

In an article originally published in *Security Journal,* George Kelling of "Broken Windows" fame, documented the successful program to rid the New York City subway of the notorious graffiti that blanketed the trains in the 1970s and early 1980s. After years of failed initiatives, the subway management adopted a fresh approach: once a car had been cleaned of graffiti it would be taken out of service and cleaned again as soon as it attracted any fresh graffiti. This removed the incentive for graffiti writers to "get up" and eventually led to the elimination of the problem.

What facilitates art graffiti?

- The proliferation of graffiti websites that provide advice and information

- Widespread availability of spray paint and other graffiti aids, including those found on the Internet

- Difficulties of apprehending and successfully prosecuting graffiti artists

- Widespread public ambivalence about the seriousness of the problem, often promoted by social commentators who may praise the activity

Examples of what has been done to address the problem

- Police and citizen surveillance teams have staked out popular graffiti-writing areas using two-way radios, home video cameras, and night vision goggles.

- Freeway signs and bridges have been secured with razor wire, and buildings protected with graffiti-resistant coatings.

- Graffiti hotlines have been established and undercover transit and police officers have been deployed in the guise of high-school students and journalists.

- High school "bounty hunters" and others have been given monetary rewards for turning in writers.

- So-called "coercive" crime prevention has been used, involving curfews from late night until sunrise (on those under the age of 18), high levels of surveillance of public areas, and extensive rules of entry and behavior in such places as shopping centers and malls.

- Writer's parents have been arrested on charges of contributing to the delinquency of minors and have been billed for thousands of dollars in damages.

- Access to spray paint and other graffiti-writing materials has been curtailed by making it a misdemeanor to sell them (the availability of these materials on the Internet could limit the value of this approach).

- Rapid cleanup has been used to deny crews the reward of having their work seen by others, thus removing the incentive for putting up graffiti (see the text boxes in this step).

- The community has been enlisted in campaigns to combat graffiti by education, community watches, beautification programs, and "paint-outs."

How can you help your agency?

A wide repertoire of measures can be deployed against graffiti crews and you can best assist your department by identifying those most appropriate for your jurisdiction. Specifically, you could:

1. Map hot spots of art graffiti, distinguish them from other graffiti hot spots, and try to predict when these locations are most likely to be hit.

2. Identify chronic offenders or crews by close study of writers' corners and "walls of fame."

3. Try to identify older, more experienced writers, who often recruit novice writers.

The NYPD's Vandal Squad concentrated on removing the most prominent graffiti artists. For big busts they spent time researching and developing a profile of the writer's identity. Since active writers were extremely secretive about their identities, the Squad often made very public arrests of older writers, therefore discouraging the younger ones.

4. Monitor websites, such as graffiti.org, that promote graffiti writing. These websites provide a wealth of information not only on individual and crew activities, but also their associates and networks. See if they include specific information about your jurisdiction.

READ MORE:

Jeff Ferrell. 1993. *Crimes of Style: Urban Graffiti and the Politics of Criminality.* Boston: Northeastern University Press.

M. Sloan-Howitt, and George Kelling. 1992. "Subway graffiti in New York City: 'Getting Up' vs. 'Meanin It and Cleanin It.'" In *Situational Crime Prevention: Successful Case Studies,* ed. R.V. Clarke. Albany, New York: Harrow and Heston. (Reprinted from *Security Journal.*)

THE HELLS ANGELS ARE THE BEST KNOWN OF ALL OUTLAW MOTORCYCLE GANGS (OMG). These are criminal organizations that are mostly involved in the distribution of illegal drugs, though they also commit other crimes, including extortion, intimidation, kidnapping, money laundering, robbery, motorcycle theft, and homicide.

The gangs are strictly hierarchical and vary in size from a single chapter to hundreds of chapters worldwide. The "Big Four" American-based OMGs are the Hells Angels, the Outlaws, the Bandidos, and the Pagans (see Table 16 on page 106). Local-level OMGs usually comprise fewer than 50 members.

Most national-level OMGs maintain criminal networks of regional and local motorcycle clubs, commonly referred to as "support," "puppet," or "duck" clubs, whose members undertake crime in support of the larger OMGs, and who are a source of new members.

The 1% gangs

In July 1947, a fight between two motorcycle gangs led to arrests and considerable publicity. One of the gangs was the "P.O.B.O.B." (Pissed Off Bastards Of Berdoo), which one year later took the name "Hells Angels." Commenting on the incident, the president of the American Motorcycle Association declared that motorcycle riders are law-abiding citizens with only 1 percent causing trouble. This marked the birth of OMGs, some of whose members now wear a diamond-shaped patch with "1%" on their "cuts."

Approximately 20,000 OMG members reside in the United States. They are white males who ride "American Iron," i.e., Harleys and Harley facsimiles with engines of at least 750cc. The early requirement of having an American-made motorcycle still exists today. Riding any other motorcycle is grounds for expulsion from the group.

OMG members are identified by their "colors" or patches, which are sewn on denim jackets or black leather vests and referred to as "cuts." The top rocker of the three-piece patch identifies the gang. The center shield is the gang's logo, some of which are legally trade-marked or copyrighted. The bottom rocker identifies the area or territory which that chapter or gang claims to control.

Patches and tattoos denote members' status. For example, the Hells Angels' Filthy Few patch indicates that the wearer has committed a murder for the organization. Its Dequiallo patch indicates that the wearer has committed an act of violence toward a person in authority or violently resisted arrest. The Big Four OMGs used to not attack police officers because they believed that the resulting heightened enforcement would cost far more than was gained. Since the mid-1980s, however, attacks on police have increased.

Most OMG chapters have clubhouses that are used for business and social gatherings. These have meeting rooms, bars, gym equipment, and garage areas. They have extensive security, including video-cameras, telephone scramblers, and 24-hour watches.

What facilitates OMG activities?

- Failure by police to identify and remove more violent members of the gang

- Failure to disrupt the gang by identifying and removing its leadership

- Failure to identify and dismantle "support," "puppet," or "duck" clubs

- Lack of criminal intelligence information sharing among jurisdictions

- Absence of bylaws prohibiting fortified clubhouses

- High demand for illegal drugs

Intelligence Analysis for Problem Solvers

Did you know?

- OMGs often confiscate property from expelled members and may brutally remove gang tattoos.

- Bikers who deal with the police or rival gangs, or are drug addicts, face expulsion or death.

- Hells Angels have a saying: "Three can keep a secret if two are dead."

- Bikers hang rival colors or police items upside down to signal disrespect.

- Outlaw bikers are bringing more discrimination and harassment suits against police.

- The Internet is the preferred means of communication for some OMGs.

Examples of what has been done regionally and nationally to deal with OMGs

A variety of national and international initiatives have been launched to deal with OMGs, such as the National Association of Chiefs of Police's (NACP) National Strategy to Combat Outlaw Motorcycle Gangs, and Interpol's Project Rockers that monitors OMGs throughout the world and shares information with member states about OMG memberships, *modus operandi*, and criminal activities. The project posts "red notices" that seek arrest of OMG members with outstanding warrants, and "green notices" that provide information on those who operate internationally.

Project Focus—run by the Criminal Intelligence Service of Canada—provides Canadian authorities with current information on OMGs to help them devise effective biker enforcement policies. The project maintains information on active gangs, location of clubhouses, and photo albums of gang colors in North America. It also collates information on known members including plates, telephone numbers, tattoos, physical descriptions, nicknames, and addresses.

Table 16. "Big Four" American-based outlaw motorcycle gangs

HELLS ANGELS
- 2,000-2,500 members in the United States and 26 other countries
- Engages in drug trafficking and a variety of other crimes such as extortion, homicide, money laundering, and motorcycle theft
- Most concentrated population in California; operates internationally

BANDIDOS
- 2,000-2,500 members in the United States and 13 other countries
- Mostly involved in drug trafficking
- Active in the Pacific, Southeastern, Southwestern, and West Central U.S. regions

OUTLAWS
- 1,700 members in the United States and 12 other countries
- Similar involvement in drug dealing and crimes as the Hells Angels
- The dominant OMG in the Great Lakes region

PAGANS
- 900 members in the United States, none outside the United States
- Cooperates with traditional organized crime groups
- Operates mostly in the Northeastern United States

What can you do?

Assist your agency's on-going investigations of OMGs by constructing a social network analysis of gang members (see Step 19), using data from surveillance and informants and, if available, from wiretaps. This will assist you in describing the hierarchy of command and therefore where your agency should focus its efforts to arrest the leadership.

What can your agency do?

Establish task forces. Many police agencies have established task forces that gather intelligence about local OMGs. For example, task force members might stake out OMG clubhouses and systematically record those entering. The task forces include a network of correctional, parole, and probation officers that give police added leverage for interviewing potential informants and witnesses.

Use undercover operations and informants. Undercover agents have been used to infiltrate OMGs. This can be dangerous and the agent might have to make significant compromises because the initiation process usually involves activities that are illegal or conflict with ethical policies of police departments. An alternative is to make use of informants, but this can also result in serious threats to their safety.

Use technology. Computer-assisted dispatch (CAD) hazards files can alert responding officers to OMG members' homes, work places, and locations visited, so that the officers can write offense or incident reports.

Be sure to share information. Placing gang members into the National Crime Information Center files will help notify investigators when police contact is made for traffic violations or when tracking gang members' activities and movements.

Seek the passage of bylaws prohibiting fortified buildings. Canadian municipalities have done this to prevent fortified buildings from being used as bunkers for OMGs. The bylaws regulate security features, such as metal doors, bullet-proof windows, surveillance towers, and security technology.

READ MORE:

National Drug Intelligence Center. 2009. *National Gang Threat Assessment, 2009*. Tallahassee, FL: National Gang Intelligence Center.

LOW-INCOME NEIGHBORHOODS, MARKED BY UNEMPLOYMENT AND VIOLENCE, ARE THE MAIN BREEDING GROUNDS FOR street gangs. These gangs are no longer confined to large cities, but are now found in suburban and rural areas. Many are engaged in drug dealing, however they could also be involved in other criminal activities, including robbery, auto theft, drive-by-shootings, and homicide. Many gang members join to make money from crime, but they also see the gang as a brotherhood or a support system, which they join to seek protection and respect.

According to the National Drug Intelligence Center, there are an estimated 900,000 street gang members across the country. States with the largest gang populations are California, Illinois, Texas, Florida, and Ohio. About 90 percent of gang members are African American or Hispanic (with a few Asian gangs) and about half are under the age of 18.

Street gangs are classified into three main groups according to size and operational reach:

1. National gangs comprise several thousand members that operate both nationally and internationally, especially in Mexico and Central America. Some of these include: Almighty Latin Kings, the Crips, the Bloods, 18th Street, Asian Boyz, and Vice Lord Nation.

2. Regional gangs are composed of several hundred to several thousand members. These include Florencia 13, Fresno Bulldogs, Latin Disciples, Tango Blast, and United Blood Nation.

3. Local gangs, also referred to as neighborhood gangs, vary greatly in size from a handful of individuals to a hundred or more members.

How are they organized?

Most gangs are loosely knit coalitions of small, autonomous cliques. Leadership of these gangs is usually decentralized and nonhierarchical. It can change rapidly and may vary by the type of gang activity; e.g., drug sales leaders may differ from "gangbanging" leaders.

The more organized gangs may have clearly defined leaders and leadership roles. These roles may include "making sure all laws and policies are being followed," "giving orders," "being the thinkers," and "making the overall decisions for the group."

In 1990, Los Angeles instituted "Operation Cul-de-Sac" in Newton, an inner-city neighborhood plagued by drug and gang activity. Barriers were installed to impede drive-by shootings and drive-up drug purchases. Foot and bicycle patrols were stepped up to suppress these crimes and to improve police-community relations. The barriers prevented cars from entering the street, or required those that entered to leave the same way. This increased the risks for shooters, because their targets would have their own guns ready when the car returned. In the two years after the barriers were installed, only one homicide was recorded, whereas in the year before seven homicides were committed in the area. Homicides were not displaced elsewhere.

Source: Ronald V. Clarke. 2005. *Closing Streets and Alleys to Reduce Crime: Should You Go Down This Road?* Problem-Oriented Guides for Police, Response Guide No.2. Washington, D.C.: U.S. Department of Justice, Office of Community Oriented Policing Services. Accessible at www.cops.usdoj.gov.

Many organized gangs hold regular meetings to collect dues and discuss any problems, as well as to enhance group cohesion, to communicate responsibilities, and disseminate information.

Gang member affiliations can be identified through "colors" (clothing and emblems), tattoos, hand signs (used within the gang), and graffiti (gang symbols on clothing, school books, backpacks, and walls).

Learn about Internet databases, such as GangNet and Cal/Gang, that allow law enforcement agencies to identify individuals involved in gangs—their names, street names, addresses, known associates, gang hand signals, vehicles, and tattoos. Cal/Gang can be accessed by law enforcement officers in California, while GangNet is used in many states and in Canada. The Orange County (California) Gang Incident Trafficking System combines traditional crime mapping and gang crime reporting. Local analysts used the system to discover that adult gang members were far more likely to be involved in violence than juvenile gang members, a crucial fact that was used to redirect the agency's gang intervention programs.

Gang members can be classified as hardcore, associate, or wannabe members. These designations are based on their criminal performance, street-smarts, incarceration experience, or abuse endured for the group. Membership is sometimes defined by age, such as "youngsters," "old gangsters," "young homies," and "old homies."

Examples of action taken against gangs

Two federal statutes are used to prosecute street gangs: the Racketeer Influenced and Corrupt Organizations (RICO) Act, and the continuing criminal enterprise (CCE) statutes of the Comprehensive Drug Abuse Prevention and Control Act of 1970. These "conspiracy" statutes allow prosecutors to present evidence of multiple criminal acts committed by various members of the gang.

Some cities, including Los Angeles, San Antonio, and Chicago, have adopted gang injunctions as a way of addressing local gang problems. These restraining orders are issued against specific gang members by the city's Attorney's Office and approved by a judge. The orders prohibit the gang members from engaging in certain activities that may range from selling drugs or possessing a weapon, to congregating in a group, being out at night, and possessing a cell phone.

The National Gang Center provides descriptions of successful anti-gang programs, and offers links to tools and databases that assist police to address the gang problems within their jurisdictions. The Center collates daily newspaper reports on national gang activity, and maintains a database of professionals working with gangs.

The Boston Gun Project is the most successful program to date in addressing gang violence (See Step 26).

What can you do?

Although your jurisdiction might have no homegrown gangs, gangs are mobile and you might have to deal with those that come from nearby cities. You can gather intelligence about their colors, signs, activities, and rivalries either directly, or from the police agencies who are dealing directly with these gangs. You should seek information to answer questions such as:

- How prevalent is the problem and how many gangs are in operation? Are they national, regional, or local gangs?

- Which of them pose a threat and what criminal activities are they engaged in?

- How many gang members can be identified? What is their demographic profile, i.e., racial/ethnic composition, age group, immigration status?

- Who are the gang leaders (if any) and what information is available about them? What information should be gathered about them?

Identify hotspots where these gangs are more likely to operate and determine whether their operations also reach larger areas. Determine whether any geographic shifts in their operations occur, and decide how this can be dealt with.

Prioritize gangs by the level of violence of their members. Then focus on the most violent groups first.

With sufficient intelligence in hand, advise your department about response strategies that would work best. These may range from completely eliminating the gang problem to dealing with the problem more effectively.

What can your agency do?

Raise awareness about the gang problem through schools and community organizations and develop partnerships with the community to gain help in addressing the problem. These partnerships should include faith-based groups, social service agencies, and other law enforcement agencies. Most programs that have shown success engaged in collaboration with a wide range of actors and have used a combination of prevention, intervention, and suppression strategies.

READ MORE:

Scott Decker. 2008. *Strategies to Address Gang Crime.* Washington, D.C.: U.S. Department of Justice, Office of Community Oriented Policing Services.

CRIMINAL RINGS ARE FREQUENTLY INVOLVED IN AUTO-ACCIDENT INSURANCE SCAMS, of which there are two main kinds: (1) staged accidents for which insurance claims are made; and (2) false injury and physical damage claims, so-called "build ups," resulting from actual accidents. These cases sometimes include "jump-ins," people who were not present at the accident but who file claims.

The groups involved may use the funds from insurance frauds for other criminal activities, such as drug trafficking. Indeed, the rings include many former drug traffickers.

The rings often hit insurers with many small claims to stay under the company's anti-fraud radar. When insurers begin to investigate such claims, they may find they are dealing with large rings with a wide reach.

According to the FBI, auto-accident frauds cost the insurance industry about $20 billion a year. Densely populated states, such as New York, New Jersey, California, Florida, and Massachusetts are among the hardest-hit. New York City is especially vulnerable.

Who is involved and how are they organized?

Auto-accident fraud rings recruit "accident victims" in two main ways:

- They use **"runners"** to recruit phony victims, often new immigrants, who are paid for participating in fake auto accidents.

- They use **"steerers"** to recruit accident victims from news reports, by visiting hospital emergency rooms and by approaching people who visit the police to collect copies of accident reports. They show these people how to profit from the accident and take them, or refer them, to clinics associated with the rings or directly operated by them.

  These clinics pad the bills with expensive and unnecessary treatments and then collect payment from the insurance company.

In response to legislation that classified insurance frauds as felonies, the rings have shifted tactics from actual to paper accidents. This is done by using information from legitimate or falsified police reports to steer patients to medical clinics.

Two common scams

Scheme 1. Load a car with people, pull in front of another car and slam on the brakes. If the expected collision ensues, the innocent party is almost always liable. Young women and the elderly are frequently targeted, the former because they are more prone to admitting fault and the latter because they are prone to becoming flustered. These scams, called "swoop and squat," sometimes target buses, where the passengers, who work with the ring, immediately report injuries and file insurance claims. Bus drivers sometimes work directly with the ring.

Scheme 2. Load two cars with people, crash the cars, call the police and say that everybody was hurt. The insurance companies are then billed for unnecessary medical procedures. Again, these schemes may also include buses.

Instead of paying people to borrow their insurance and their cars, the rings may use false identities to purchase cars and insurance, and, therefore, to file false insurance claims.

Factors contributing to auto-accident insurance fraud

- Ordinary citizens who are willing to participate in the schemes, because they believe that: (1) they are entitled to compensation for money they have paid in policy premiums; (2) the frauds only hurt insurance companies who deserve to be "hit"

- Lack of insurance staff trained to detect fraudulent claims

- Lack of public awareness programs to educate potential victims

- Lack of state insurance fraud bureaus that can undertake cross-jurisdictional investigations

What has been done nationally to address the problem?

In 1976, Florida passed the False and Fraudulent Insurance Claims Act (FFICA), which made insurance fraud a specific offense. Florida also created the Division of Insurance Fraud to investigate frauds falling under the definitions of the FFICA. Since then, many other states have established similar insurance fraud bureaus.

The National Insurance Crime Bureau (NICB) was formed in 1992 by over 1,000 member insurance companies to help deal with insurance fraud. The NICB serves as a conduit between the insurance industry and federal, state, and local law enforcement agencies. It holds multiple databases, currently with more than 350 million records of suspicious claims, which insurance companies can access to check claims.

A successful prosecution

In November 2000, the Federal District Court in Brooklyn broke up a 53-member auto insurance fraud ring that cheated insurance companies out of more than $1 million by staging 27 crashes in New York City. Two employees of Medical Arts Rehabilitation clinic led the ring. They paid people $500 to stage an accident. These people recruited new drivers and passengers to crash their own cars, who were treated at the clinic for injuries that were never sustained. The clinic then billed insurance companies for up to $20,000 for medical services, while the passengers filed bodily injury claims for between $3,000 and $22,000. Many of the recruits were "unsophisticated and often recent arrivals to the United States."

Source: Alan Feuer. 2000. Car Crashes Were Staged For Fraud, U.S. Charges. *New York Times,* November 17.

Most insurance companies subscribe to the American Insurance Services Group Index, which provides data pertaining to bodily injury and workers' compensation. Many have established hotlines with interactive conversation that allows for the gathering of detailed information about possible insurance fraud claims. Many have also established Special Investigative Units (SIU) specifically to investigate possible fraudulent claims.

Randolph (Massachusetts) P.D. partnered with other state and county law enforcement entities to form the Community Insurance Fraud Initiative (CIFI), a task force to address the city's auto insurance fraud problem. The CIFI offered a $5,000 reward for information leading to the arrest and conviction of perpetrators of the fraud. Two hundred and sixty-three individuals were arrested, which, together with arrests made by other task forces operating in six nearby cities, resulted in a reduction of $100 million in fake auto accident claims in those cities in 2004.

What can you do?

Gather information on the time and location of auto-accidents, as well as the number of people involved in each accident to determine if possible rings are involved. Staged auto-accidents happen during busy times on busy streets, and generally involve many passengers.

Determine if there is a high concentration of auto accidents in neighborhoods or areas with high concentrations of immigrant populations. Gather information about the people involved in the accidents, including their age, gender, and ethnicity, which may help determine whether staged accidents are taking place.

Learn how to use the different databases provided by NICB designed to fight insurance fraud. The wealth of knowledge provided by this organization can prove valuable in your department's investigative efforts.

What can your agency do?

Coordinate fraud probes with the insurance companies as well as other law enforcement agencies—such as the Attorney General's office, district attorneys, or U.S. attorneys—as the problem may require a multi-jurisdictional approach.

Deploy undercover officers posing as accident victims to probe unscrupulous medical clinics that pad claims. Determine if these clinics work with an auto-insurance fraud ring and try to infiltrate their operations.

Execute wiretaps to gather information from medical clinics, lawyers, and employees of the insurance company suspected of involvement in the ring.

Work closely with community organizations and immigrant groups to educate them about the dangers and risks involved in taking part in staged auto accidents.

READ MORE:

Tony Baldock. 1997. *Insurance Fraud*. Trends and Issues in Crime and Criminal Justice, No. 66. Australian Institute of Criminology.

ORGANIZED SHOPLIFTERS STEAL LARGE AMOUNTS OF MERCHANDISE FOR RESALE. They may operate across state lines, and may target the same chain in different places. Their arrival in your town might be signaled by a spike in reports of goods being shoplifted in large quantities.

The groups are frequently composed of immigrants (legal or not) from the Middle East, South America, or Asia. This may be because they can sell the goods they steal to fellow immigrants who run small businesses. The groups sometimes also take part in drug trafficking, car theft, and burglary.

The FBI reports that organized retail theft costs businesses $12–$35 billion annually in stolen goods, lost sales, and replacement costs. It is believed that the profits from organized shoplifting are sometimes used to fund foreign terrorists; according to the CRISP report (in the Read more section), "money laundering has been proven in many, if not all, organized retail crime rings operated by Middle Easterners."

How are they organized?

Each group consists of several members with distinct roles: "boosters" steal the goods; "handlers" sell the goods to fences; and others take care of transport and logistics.

Boosters act alone or in groups. They steal large quantities at one time, usually of the same items. They carry tools to remove security tags, they use foil-lined bags to defeat electronic tags, and they may use cell phones to communicate with other group members while shoplifting. They may change bar codes so merchandise registers at a much lower price on checkout ("ticket switching"). They may use stolen credit cards and use the receipts to return stolen goods to the store for cash. In some cases, they may simply wheel carts full of merchandise out the doors to a waiting getaway van.

The stolen property may be held in rented storage units before being taken to the group's home base. The property is often sold to *street-level fences*, who might own a bodega, pawnshop, or gas station. Some fences operate from home, selling items door-to-door, in flea markets and local taverns, or even on the Internet. They might sell-on the goods to *mid-level fences*, who clean and repackage them to look like new and then sell them to *wholesale diverters*, who might mix them with legitimate goods for sale to retailers.

What facilitates the work of organized shoplifters?

- Their unexpected arrival in towns and cities and equally quick departure

- Their links with immigrant communities, which facilitate disposal of goods

- Complacent retailers who have not been victimized by organized shoplifters

- Low priority accorded by police, prosecutors, and judges to shoplifting and fencing operations

- Poor security in many stores that puts them at risk (see below)

Which stores are at risk?

1. Those that sell goods that are CRAVED (concealable, removable, available, valuable, enjoyable, and disposable). Designer clothing, over-the-counter medicine, electronics, DVDs, health and beauty supplies, razor blades and infant formulas are considered to be among the "hot products" targeted by organized shoplifters in supermarkets.

2. Large stores that make it easier for organized groups to hide among ordinary shoppers

3. Stores located close to highways that provide easy escape routes

4. Stores with many part-time associates who have less commitment, lack theft awareness, and have limited training

5. Stores with the security weaknesses that aid ordinary shoplifters (see *Shoplifting, 2nd Edition,* Problem-Oriented Policing Guide No 11). Such weaknesses include:

   a. Lax return policies that allow thieves to return stolen items to the store for credit or cash

   b. Unmonitored exits, blind corners/spots, high displays that conceal thieves from view, and open displays of high-risk items

   c. No security staff, poor stocktaking, and lacking security equipment such as electronic article surveillance and video-cameras

6. Stores that do not report shoplifting to the police

What is being done regionally and nationally?

Walmart, Target®, Lowe's®, Limited Brands, and other large retailers seek to identify organized shoplifting rings by investing in software that tracks regional patterns of theft.

Many states have passed laws that address organized retail crime and, in 2009, Congress passed the Combating Organized Retail Crime Act and the E-fencing Enforcement Act.

The Law Enforcement Retail Partnership database (LERPnet) was created for merchants to share information on organized shoplifting with local, state, and federal law enforcement, as well as with other retailers.

What can you do?

Regularly scan for stores with high shoplifting rates (see Table 17 on page 116) and try to determine the reasons. Notify your supervisors about the need to alert the stores to their problematic status and the need to take preventive actions. Keep in mind that reported shoplifting may be significantly lower than actual shoplifting due to differences in store security policies and staffing.

Alert other analysts and police officers to signs of organized shoplifting.

What can your agency do?

Work with local merchants to encourage reporting of shoplifting and early sharing of information about the arrival of an organized crime shoplifting group. Alert nearby jurisdictions to the possible arrival of these groups in their locations.

Educate retailers about theft prevention and the importance of reporting shoplifting incidents. Measures focused on organized shoplifting include: displays that prevent the removal of multiple packages at one time; cabinets that beep if open too long; and stamping the store's name on over-the-counter medicines or infant formula cans to reduce their re-sale value.

Reduce the opportunities to dispose of stolen goods by regularly monitoring pawnshops, flea markets, and used-goods stores. Visit local bodegas, taverns, and other small businesses, especially those owned by recent immigrants, to ask about suspicious attempts to sell them goods.

READ MORE:

Ronald Clarke and Gohar Petrossian. 2012. *Shoplifting 2nd Edition. Problem-Oriented Guides for Police. Problem-Specific Guides Series, No. 11.* Washington, D.C.: U.S. Department of Justice, Office of Community Oriented Policing Services.

Walter Palmer and Chris Richardson. 2009. *Organized Retail Crime: Assessing the Risk and Developing Effective Strategies.* ASIS International Foundation CRISP Report.

Table 17. Reported shoplifting by store in Danvers, Massachusetts

> **Scan regularly for stores with high rates of shoplifting.** Crime analyst Christopher Bruce did this for the Danvers (Massachusetts) Police and produced this table. The store with the most shoplifting incidents was one of the largest in the town. But when size was taken into account by calculating the number of thefts per 1,000 square feet (see the final column of the table), the riskiest store turned out to be the one that had been ranked 3rd on the list before correcting for size; it was a tiny boutique store with staggeringly high shoplifting.
>
> Visit the riskiest stores and try to understand why their rates of shoplifting are so high and what they might do to reduce the risks.

REPORTED SHOPLIFTING BY STORE IN DANVERS, MASSACHUSETTS, NOVEMBER 2008 TO OCTOBER 2010					
Store	Thefts	Percent of All Thefts	Cumulative % Thefts	Cumulative % Stores	Thefts Per 1,000 Sq. Ft.
1	210	33%	33%	2%	2.06
2	152	24%	56%	3%	1.83
3	36	6%	62%	5%	144.00
4	29	5%	67%	6%	0.36
5	24	4%	70%	8%	0.32
6	23	4%	74%	10%	0.28
7	21	3%	77%	11%	0.26
8	15	2%	80%	13%	0.18
9	9	1%	81%	14%	0.11
10	9	1%	82%	16%	0.11
11	9	1%	84%	17%	0.14
12	6	1%	85%	19%	20.00
13	6	1%	86%	21%	0.10
14	5	1%	86%	22%	0.17
15	5	1%	87%	24%	0.07
16	5	1%	88%	25%	0.13
17	5	1%	89%	27%	3.13
46 Stores with <5 Thefts	72	11%	100%	100%	

TEMPORARY THEFT OF CARS, OFTEN COMMITTED BY JUVENILE JOYRIDERS OR, TO A LESSER EXTENT, FOR USE OF THE car in committing another crime, accounts for the bulk of car thefts. Permanent thefts, where the car is never recovered, are often committed by organized criminals, who are employing increasingly sophisticated tactics to outsmart today's anti-theft devices. These thefts account for the bulk of the costs of car theft. In 2011, 47.7 percent of the value of the vehicles stolen was never recovered according to UCR reports, causing losses of about $1.8 billion nationwide.

Several forms of permanent theft exist, including:

- "Rebirthing," which is giving the car a new identity for resale

- "Chopping" the car and selling its parts

- Exporting the car, which is accomplished by shipping it overseas from one of the nation's many sea ports or driving it over the border to Mexico

You should try to determine if a car theft ring is operating in your area, and whether the cars are stolen for export. Theft for export is particularly likely if you are close to the Mexico border or near a major port. This step describes two techniques that will assist you in this task. It does not describe the facilitating conditions for organized car theft, or the *modus operandi* involved, since these are used for illustrative purposes in Step 10, "Modify the conditions that facilitate organized crimes," and Step 11, "Study the *modus operandi* step-by-step."

Compare your auto theft rates with those of other jurisdictions

Officers in Chula Vista (California) P.D. suspected that being close to the Mexican border exacerbated the city's auto theft problem. The department's crime analysts tested this idea by calculating the theft rates for Chula Vista and neighboring cities. They found that Chula Vista's auto theft rates, and those of other cities closest to the border, were two to six times higher than ones further north in San Diego County (see Figure 17). Many vehicles were stolen from parking lots and driven across the border before owners had even discovered the thefts. The analysts also found that pick-up trucks—highly prized in Mexico—were at greatest risk, and that the recovery rates of these trucks stolen in Chula Vista were lower than in cities further from the border.

Organized car theft on the U.S./Mexico border

Resendiz has described a division of labor among those involved in the export of stolen vehicles from the United States to Mexico:

Chauffeurs provided vehicles to cruise around mall parking lots and residential areas to "shop" for possible target vehicles.

Specialists used different tools to steal different model vehicles. They used flat head screwdrivers and vise grips to open Chevrolets, master keys for Chryslers, dent-pullers, screwdrivers, and vise grips for Fords. They usually took between fifteen seconds to one and a half minutes to break into any car.

Mounters were responsible for driving the vehicle to the buyers in Mexico. Once the vehicle was crossed, it was dropped off at a designated hideout, and from there, to customers and buyers.

Source: Rosalva Resendiz. 1998. International Auto Theft: An Exploratory Research of Organization and Organized Crime on the U.S./Mexico Border. *Criminal Organizations* 12:25–30.

Calculate location quotients to identify a possible theft for export problem

The fact that many vehicles are stolen in your area may not mean that organized car thieves are operating; it could simply reflect a generally high rate of crime in your area. To test this you can calculate a Crime Location Quotient (CLQ). A CLQ compares the total number of a particular crime across a set of geographical units (for example, neighborhoods, cities, or counties), taking into account the distribution of other crimes in those units (see Figure 18 for an example of the calculations). It is the ratio of target crimes to all crimes in a jurisdiction (e.g., county) divided by the ratio of the target crimes to all crimes in a larger area (e.g., state).

Figure 18. CLQ calculation to estimate the prevalence of theft for export in U.S. counties

Researchers have recently used the CLQ calculation to estimate the prevalence of theft for export in U.S. counties.

They used the following formula:

CLQ= (a/b)/(X/Y)

a= total number of motor vehicle thefts within the county

b= total number of all index crimes within the county

X= total number of motor vehicle thefts within the state where the county is located

Y= total number of all index crimes within that state

A CLQ value of 1.00 indicates an area has a typical representation of that crime compared to all other crimes. CLQ s over 1.00 indicate overrepresentation of a particular crime, while CLQ values under 1.00 signify underrepresentation.

The map shows that theft for export is prevalent near heavily-trafficked borders and ports in the United States.

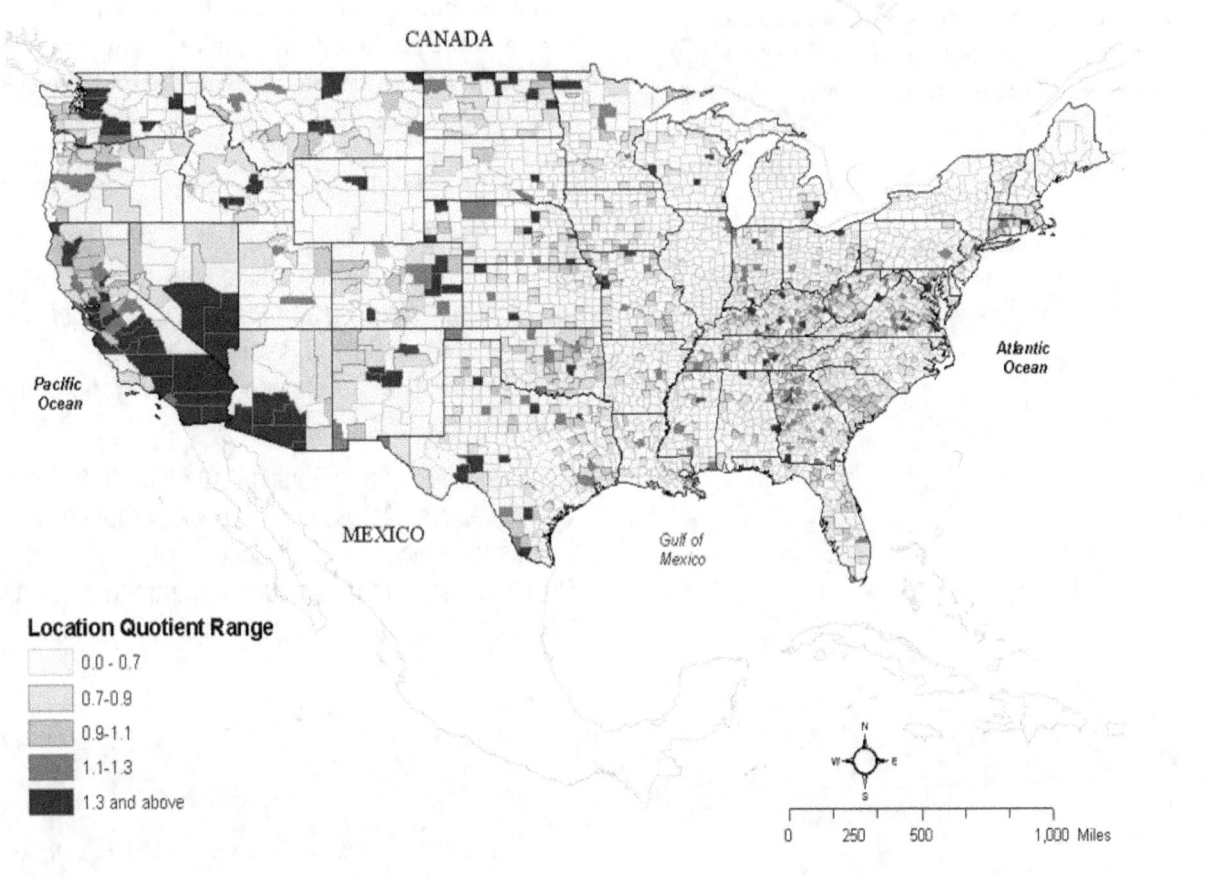

Location Quotients for Motor Vehicle Theft for Continental U.S. by County, 2007

Location Quotient Range
- 0.0 - 0.7
- 0.7-0.9
- 0.9-1.1
- 1.1-1.3
- 1.3 and above

What has been done to prevent theft for export?

Anything that makes it harder to steal a car will slow down the work of organized car theft rings, especially of the less sophisticated operators. Over the years, a wide variety of measures have been introduced to increase the risks or difficulty of car theft, including improvements to vehicle security, parking facilities, and vehicle documentation procedures. (In recent years, very promising reductions in theft have been reported for vehicles fitted with electronic immobilizers at manufacture—which is now a requirement for all new vehicles in the European Union, Canada, and Australia, but not yet in the United States.) In addition, some other measures specifically intended to reduce theft for export have been introduced, such as:

- The United States has developed a model bilateral agreement for the repatriation of stolen vehicles and has signed agreements with numerous countries in Latin America. U.S. agents have provided training to customs officials in these countries in ways to identify stolen cars.

- The National Insurance Crime Bureau has assisted these efforts by stationing officials in Mexico and other South American countries to assist the process of repatriation.

- U.S. Customs is field testing portable, hand-held computer scanners that will give inspectors in the field instant access to VIN information, as well as identify vehicles previously presented for export.

- X-ray machines that can detect vehicles concealed in containers are increasingly being deployed at major U.S. sea ports.

- Many local programs encourage citizens to participate in vehicle theft prevention. For example, a program implemented by the McAllen (Texas) P.D., "Citizens Against Auto Theft," involved placing colored decals on windows of automobiles. This alerted law enforcement officials that the car is not to be driven during certain hours of the day or driven into Mexico.

What can your agency do?

Should your analyses suggest that a theft for export ring is operating in your jurisdiction, your agency could implement a program such as that developed by McAllen P.D. Publicizing the problem can be another option. By analyzing your vehicle theft records you can determine which makes and models are at most risk, and the public information campaigns can be geared toward encouraging owners of these vehicles to better secure their cars.

READ MORE:

Nancy Plouffe and Rana Sampson. 2004. "Auto Theft and Theft from Autos in Parking Lots in Chula Vista, CA." In *Understanding and Preventing Car Theft*, ed., Michael G. Maxfield and Ronald V. Clarke. Vol. 17 of *Crime Prevention Studies*. Monsey, New York: Criminal Justice Press.

Gohar Petrossian and Ronald V. Clarke. 2012. *Export of Stolen Vehicles Across Land Borders*. Problem-Oriented Guides for Police. Problem-Specific Guides Series, No. 63. Washington, D.C.: U.S. Department of Justice, Office of Community Oriented Policing Services.

METHAMPHETAMINE IS SUPPLIED BY TWO MAIN TYPES OF NETWORKS: (1) large, highly organized groups involved in trafficking illicit drugs, and (2) smaller, less organized groups of individuals typically involved in methamphetamine use.

The laboratories that produce methamphetamine have changed over time. There are now three main types of clandestine operations in the United States, which vary in organization, size, and production capacity: (1) super labs, (2) mom-and-pop labs, and (3) shake-and-bake or one pot labs. Shake-and-bake labs are the newest and most common type of production method. The shake-and-bake method can produce methamphetamine in about 30 minutes in a plastic bottle.

Clandestine laboratories today are primarily ephedrine and pseudoephedrine based. Most local laboratories in the United States are run by small networks of methamphetamine users and low-level dealers. Group members may coordinate efforts to acquire necessary supplies and chemicals. Restricted precursor chemicals may be obtained by "smurfing," whereby numerous individuals visit multiple retail outlets to make pseudoephedrine purchases. Group members also recruit others to purchase pseudoephedrine. Smurfing activities are increasing and evolving to include the illicit acquisition of bulk quantities of pseudoephedrine.

Clandestine laboratories are hazardous, toxic, and volatile. They are located in a variety of settings including homes, motel rooms, or vehicles. Smaller laboratories are portable and more difficult to detect. While laboratories were traditionally located in specific regions and in rural communities, they are now being found in cities across the United States. According to the DEA, 118,940 clandestine laboratories have been seized in the United States since 2004. Given that law enforcement detects a small percentage of labs, the true number is unknown.

Who is involved and how are they organized?

The groups involved in producing methamphetamine in clandestine laboratories continue to change as the problem evolves. Groups adapt to control efforts and may alter the way they communicate, acquire chemicals and supplies, and produce methamphetamine.

A successful prosecution

A federal prosecution in U.S. District court resulted in the conviction of 13 persons for conspiracy to manufacture methamphetamine. The defendants were charged with collecting chemicals needed to produce methamphetamine from multiple states for production purposes. The group was involved with producing methamphetamine in multiple locations including the home of a 60-year-old defendant. Sentences ranged from 3 years to 20 years.

Source: Todd South. 2012. 13-Person Meth Case Ends with Sentencing. *Chattanooga Times Free Press*, June 23.

Groups may be small (2–4 people) and loosely organized, or larger with more organization. They may be headed by independent operators or in conjunction with criminal gangs. Members may be recruited for specific roles related to manufacturing, including:

- Gathering supplies
- Purchasing precursor chemicals
- Recruiting others to purchase precursors
- Assisting with production
- Distributing methamphetamine

Cash or drugs may be exchanged for assistance. While local production is dominated by small and transient groups, larger, more organized groups have recently become involved in production in California.

Meth supply: at every step, offenders adapt, markets shift, and supply continues

The U.S. methamphetamine supply serves as an example of the challenges of responding to complex and evolving crime problems. Despite decades of attempts to control the supply of methamphetamine, clandestine production and trafficking continues and methamphetamine is widely available. Local manufacturers have continually adapted to control efforts by discovering alternative methods of production. Reductions in local supply are regularly offset by increases in production and trafficking from Mexico. There is need to develop a better understanding of the processes that underlie offender adaptation and offending evolution at local, national, and international levels.

Factors contributing to clandestine manufacturing

- Continuing demand for methamphetamine
- Profitability
- Increased use of smurfing to acquire bulk quantities of pseudoephedrine
- Retail outlets that sell pseudoephedrine products without questioning suspicious purchases
- Continuous adaptations in manufacturing production processes

What has been done nationally to address the problem?

In 2005, the U.S. Government passed the U.S.A. Patriot Improvement and Reauthorization Act. This legislation restricted retail access to pseudoephedrine, placed limitations on the purchase quantities, enhanced penalties for offenders, and increased regulations for distributors. Individual states have enacted various laws aimed at restricting access to precursors, criminalizing manufacturing-related activities, and increasing punishments. In 2006, Oregon became the first state in the United States to require a prescription for pseudoephedrine.

What can you do?

Conduct an in-depth analysis of the methamphetamine problem. Assess each dimension of the broader problem (i.e., use, trafficking, and manufacturing).

Data on drug treatment admissions are available from Substance Abuse and Mental Health Services Administration on the Treatment Episode Data Set (TEDS) website. Data on arrests, convictions, and sentences of criminal offenders can be obtained from criminal justice agencies.

Determine whether methamphetamine is being manufactured locally, imported, or both. Identify how much of the methamphetamine on the streets is being produced locally versus being trafficked in from out of state or out of the country.

If local production is occurring, gather information on the following:

- Type(s) of production processes being utilized
- Type(s) of laboratories producing methamphetamine
- The main ingredients being used
- Where offenders are obtaining ingredients and supplies
- How are offenders are obtaining precursor chemicals both legally and illicitly

Create a record of clandestine lab seizures and analyze this data to identify trends in production at the local level.

Review logs of local pseudoephedrine sales for suspicious patterns of purchases and to determine if certain retail outlets are selling disproportionately high rates of pseudoephedrine.

Look for information everywhere. You may need to talk to law enforcement officers, review police reports, and discuss the issue with community members who may have special knowledge about the problem. This could include pharmacists, persons who work in farming communities where anhydrous ammonia is available, and personnel employed at stores where other chemicals and supplies needed to manufacture methamphetamine are sold. Understanding which communities have high rates of methamphetamine consumption and how many individuals with previous involvement in manufacturing or related activities reside in the area will be helpful.

What can your agency do?

Gather intelligence on clandestine manufacturing from confidential informants and by sharing information with other law enforcement agencies in the area. Intelligence sharing is essential for obtaining information on suspicious patterns of activity that may cross jurisdictional boundaries.

Coordinate investigations with other law enforcement agencies.

Conduct undercover surveillance operations in retail outlets that sell pseudoephedrine in communities known to have high rates of methamphetamine use or that sell disproportionately high rates of pseudoephedrine products.

READ MORE:

Rashi Shukla, Jordan Crump, and Emelia Chrisco. 2012. An Evolving Problem: Methamphetamine Production and Trafficking in the United States. *International Journal of Drug Policy* 23:426–435.

Michael Scott and Kelly Dedel. 2006. *Clandestine Methamphetamine Labs*, 2nd Edition. Problem-Oriented Guides for Police. Problem-Specific Guides Series, No 16. Washington, D.C.: U.S. Department of Justice, Office of Community Oriented Policing Services.

44

ON WEEKEND EVENINGS, CITY CENTER PUBS IN BRITAIN ARE CROWDED BY YOUNG MEN AND WOMEN who are there to see and to be seen. In Mediterranean countries, especially on warm evenings, the same demographic groups fill the cafes and stroll on the piazza. In North America, late on fine evenings in spring and summer, young people, sometimes in the hundreds or even thousands, "cruise" the local strip in their automobiles, driving slowly, bumper-to-bumper.

Cruising is a means for young men to show off their cars, to compare them with other people's cars, to find racing competitors, to socialize, and to impress young women. In many communities across the country cruising is considered a pastime and a rite of passage, encouraged and glorified by movies like *American Graffiti* and *The Hollywood Knights*. According to a 2002 survey conducted by Teenage Research Unlimited, 60 percent of teenagers spent at least four hours a week cruising in a car. Another survey of young cruisers between the ages of 19 to 21 revealed that 80 percent of the time their parents knew and approved of their cruising in the downtown area. It seems that parents preferred the downtown area because of the supervision of patrol officers.

On the other hand, cruising can bring many problems in its wake. It snarls traffic, it can prevent access by emergency vehicles, and it can bring commerce to a halt. It may also bring problems of litter, urinating in public, underage drinking, vandalism, and worse. It is these consequences of cruising that the police need to address, not the otherwise harmless behavior of ordinary young men and women looking for social interaction.

Cruising is generally confined to downtown areas, though in coastal communities it is common along beaches. Cruisers drive a wide range of cars that include classic cars (whose drivers tend to be older and cruise to show off their expensively restored vehicles); pickup trucks (on huge wheels and jacked up suspensions); mini-trucks, muscle cars, low riders (whose chassis ride just inches off the ground); imported customized European cars; and Harley-Davidson motorcycles.

Factors contributing to cruising

- Automobile ownership and accessibility to teenagers

- The need to be socially accepted

- The desire to show off vehicles

- Many cruisers are too young to go to bars or other places where they can socialize with friends and the opposite sex

- An unsupervised environment where youth can express themselves

What has been done nationally to address the problem?

The Salt Lake City Council in Utah passed an anti-cruising ordinance prohibiting cars from driving repeatedly (defined as driving three or more times in the same direction) past a "mobile traffic-control point" between 11:00 PM and 4:00 AM in an area identified by police as being congested.

Police in Lakewood, Colorado, employed a strategy of "modified diversion" by closing off known cruising locations during 8:00 PM and 2:00 AM, the time period when cruising was most likely to occur, while minimizing its impact on legitimate traffic and businesses in these areas. The closing was announced through a news media campaign, which began a week in advance of the operation. This effort resulted in complete elimination of the cruising problem in Lakewood.

When the enforcement strategies and the use of barriers failed to solve the cruising problem in Arlington, Texas, the police formed a "cruising committee" by forging partnerships with representatives of the city council, local business owners, and the parks, recreation, and transport

Santa Ana Cruising Abatement Project

The Santa Ana Police Department in California was faced with a serious cruising problem. On Sunday evenings, approximately 1,000 cruisers drove along a major thoroughfare to gather and socialize. The cruising night resembled a large street party, where loud music and alcohol consumption were common, creating problems for nearby residents. Merchants complained that traffic gridlock kept regular customers from their businesses, and many businesses closed early to avoid subjecting their customers to intimidation from the cruisers. The police department responded to the problem by focusing on two weaknesses of the cruisers: (a) they lacked knowledge of anti-cruising laws, and (b) many of the cruisers drove vehicles belonging to their parents or others. The police set up a control point, where information about each vehicle was quickly made available through specially-designed computer software. At the same time, officers distributed an anti-cruising warning to each vehicle moving through the check point. The contact with the drivers was intended to reduce anonymity. Follow-up letters were then mailed to the registered owners of the vehicles advising them that the car had been identified as cruising, an illegal activity in Santa Ana. The letter was intended to warn cruisers who drove their own vehicles, and to inform parents whose cars were being used by their children. The letter warned that anyone who returned to the area to cruise would be subject to arrest. The check points, as well as roadblocks leading to these points were eliminated after several weeks. The project proved to be successful in reducing cruising and related problems in the area.

departments, which leased a downtown parking lot on Friday and Saturday nights and opened it to the cruisers. It was staffed by police, equipped with portable restrooms and cleaned up the next morning. The approach proved highly effective, as it not only solved the cruising problem, but also helped reduce other related problems. Up to 1,000 cars continued to cruise there during an evening, but local people had no longer to endure litter, vandalism, noise, and other public order problems.

What can you do?

If cruising is a problem in your jurisdiction, you can gather information about the characteristics of the cruisers and determine if they are engaged in problematic behaviors that stem from cruising.

Map the locations as well as the days of the week and time of the day when cruising is most likely to occur. Gather as much information as possible about these temporal and geographic patterns. Think about possible interventions you could advise based on successful actions in other jurisdictions. Help your department find an alternative location for cruising that would lead to fewer problems but which would still be used by the young people.

What can your agency do?

Find out more about cruising by surveying local residents and businesses. Engage them in efforts to address the problem.

Once the cruising areas and times are identified, your department may increase enforcement in these areas during these designated times. Leaving aside arrests or citations for cruising, the presence of the police may reduce other related problems in the area.

Find an alternative cruising area that appeals to the cruisers and does not conflict with the area businesses or the residents. This area can be controlled by the officers to ensure security.

READ MORE:

Boise Police Department Planning Unit. 1990. *Downtown 'Cruising' In Major U.S. Cities and One City's Response to the Problem.* Boise, Idaho: Police Department.

Ron W. Glensor and Kenneth J. Peak. 2005. *Cruising.* Problem-Oriented Guides for Police. Problem-Specific Guides Series, No. 29. Washington, D.C.: U.S. Department of Justice, Office of Community Oriented Policing Services.

45

SOME STREET RACERS ARE WELL-OFF STUDENTS, MOTOR SPORT ENTHUSIASTS, AND EVEN MIDDLE-AGED BUSINESSMEN, but the three main groups are:

1. Young working-class males aged 16–25, some of whom attend trade schools or technical colleges, but many may have struggled in school and engaged in other delinquency. Most members of this group quite soon grow out of street racing.

2. Older white males (aged 25–40) who race older American-made "muscle" cars, such as Corvettes, Camaros, and Mustangs.

3. A wide age range of Asian and Hispanic males who generally drive later-model Japanese cars, such as Hondas, Acuras, Mitsubishis, and Nissans. This group currently dominates the street racing scene.

Races test a driver's skill and the capabilities of the vehicles involved. They often take place at night in largely deserted streets or industrial areas. Street racing is not illegal in some jurisdictions, but it tends to be associated with illegal activities, including auto theft, impaired driving, illegal vehicle modification, illicit gambling, gang related activity, trespassing, vandalism, and littering. Fatal crashes linked to street racing have been found to involve both alcohol and excessive speed and often occur on urban surface streets.

How are they organized?

Street races are often publicized by word of mouth and may be attended by dozens of racers and hundreds of spectators. During the race, lookouts keep watch for police using cell phones, police scanners, and walkie-talkies. Some groups may use police tape and false signs to block traffic for the duration of the race, or use rolling road-blocks to stage a race on a large highway.

In some cases, illegal racers may operate websites to post announcements about race locations and about expected police activity. Some websites provide information about the previous night's races, including ratings of police presence and crowd size. They may carry a link to the local police agency so the curious can see if a warrant has been issued for their arrest.

Forms of street racing

■ **Drag racing** involves a contest between two vehicles that compete to cross a set finish line. In some jurisdictions drag racing is classified as a Class B misdemeanor. According to the National Highway Traffic Safety Administration, about 135 people die each year in street drag racing accidents.

■ **Hat Racing**, also called "cannonball run" or "kamikaze," involves point-to-point races where drivers put money into a hat for the winner. These races are often long distance, sometimes from city to city.

■ **Touge** or **Centipede** races, popularized in Japan, occur on mountain passes or around normal traffic, one car at a time, or chase-style with a convoy of vehicles.

■ **Burnouts** involve spinning rear tires at high revolutions to produce smoke trails.

■ **Donuts** involve accelerating a vehicle with full steering-wheel lock.

■ **Rolling Road Blockages** or **Blockades** comprise vehicles traveling slowly in convoy on major highways to prevent other vehicles from passing, so that vehicles ahead can engage in racing.

■ **Drifting** involves accelerating around a corner to cause the rear of the vehicle to slide out and the tires to slip on the roadway.

Factors contributing to illegal street racing

- Availability of vehicles to young drivers

- Lack of legitimate venues for racing and the existence of suitable abandoned or unsupervised locations

- The need for thrills and excitement, as well as the expression of masculinity

- Street racers' need for social status

- Existence of street racing movies and video clips on the Internet that can be imitated

- Lack of ordinances prohibiting street racing

- The support of spectators

Examples of what has been done to address the problem

Kent (Washington) Police Department partnered with other law enforcement agencies, private property owners, local businesses, and the insurance industry to develop an enforcement plan known as CRASH (Curb Racing and Achieve Safer Highways). Police conducted surveillance of racing locations to identify races in progress and, once identified, uniformed officers closed off exits from the locations to prevent participants from dispersing. Drivers operating vehicles in violation of the traffic code were cited or arrested. Vehicles operated by drivers whose licenses had been suspended or revoked were impounded.

Some jurisdictions have installed speed bumps, concrete barricades, and freeway billboards to control or inform racers. To discourage spectators, parking can be prohibited on public properties and roadways during prime racing hours in the race area.

Australia and New Zealand have addressed street racing through legislation directed at such activities as dangerous or careless driving, causing unnecessary noise and smoke as a result of "burnouts," and causing deliberate loss of traction doing "donuts." Drivers who take part in these behaviors can have their operator's license suspended and face the immediate impounding of their vehicles for periods of 48 hours to three months. Subsequent offenses may result in forfeiture of vehicles.

San Diego has acted to curb its street racing problem

- By passing a "spectator ordinance" making it an offense to attend an illegal street-racing event, and a "forfeiture ordinance" permitting the police to seize vehicles used in races.

- By establishing "DragNet," a special unit to deal with the races. Officers infiltrate the illegal street-racing group to videotape races and use driver and license plate information to arrest the offenders.

- By designating the Qualcomm Stadium as a location for races, held on Friday nights.

Annual street races are permitted in cities in Canada (Toronto and Montreal) and Australia (Sydney, Adelaide, and Melbourne). This allows racers to experience the fun, camaraderie, and excitement they seek within a safer racing environment. Police can either work with existing national programs (Beat the Heat, Racers Against Street Racing, the National Hot Rod Association) that encourage safe, on-track racing, or implement their own local program.

What can you do?

Determine whether you have an illegal street racing problem in your jurisdiction. If so, study the characteristics of the racers, the kinds of activities they are involved in, and who their supporters are.

Inform yourself about street racing through websites, such as Streetracing.com, RaceLegal.com and NHRA. com. These websites provide racing and club news, articles, calendars, chat rooms, auctions, and message boards for many cities and states. The NHRA website focuses on encouraging legal racing, and attempts to educate users about related laws and statistics, such as number of illegal racers who were recently killed, injured, cited, arrested, or who had vehicles seized or licenses revoked.

Through the chat rooms provided by these websites, you might be able to warn your department about upcoming races in your jurisdiction. Using network analysis you might be able to build up a picture of the major players involved in the groups. You can also infiltrate and monitor social networking sites to remain informed about upcoming street racing events.

What can your agency do?

Inform parents about the dangers of street racing so they can discourage their teenagers from participating. Ask parents to inform police about possible future street races that they hear about from their teenagers.

Place roadblocks leading to locations where street racing is most likely to occur. These locations should be supervised during prime hours for street racing.

Study solutions adopted elsewhere—in particular whether legal venues for street racing can be created, which can be more easily monitored and controlled.

READ MORE:

Ron Glensor and Kenneth Peak. 2004. *Street Racing. Problem-Oriented Guides for Police.* Problem-Specific Guides Series, No. 28.Washington, D.C.: U.S. Department of Justice, Office of Community Oriented Policing Services.

46 SPRING BREAKS

THE ROOTS OF THE "SPRING BREAK" TRADITION CAN BE TRACED BACK TO THE FIRST COLLEGE SWIM FORUM, held in Fort Lauderdale in 1938. Since then, "spring break" has become a rite of passage among young college students across North America. It gained prominence through such films as *Where the Boys Are* (1960) and *Spring Break* (1983) and has been further popularized through MTV's "Spring Break" and the video series "Girls Gone Wild." Also, an industry of promoters of spring break trips advertise on college campuses.

Approximately half a million students each year vacation at popular spring break destinations. These include South Padre Island, Texas; Palm Springs, California; Fort Lauderdale, Daytona Beach, Pensecola, and Panama City Beach, Florida; and Lake Havasu, Arizona. Recent years have also seen increased numbers of students taking spring breaks in foreign destinations that include Cancun, Matzalan, and Acapulco, Mexico; as well as the Bahamas and Jamaica. Younger students may go to Mexico because of the lower legal drinking age of 18.

Students on spring break often engage in heavy alcohol consumption/binge drinking and some recreational drug use. One study at Panama City Beach found that an average male student had 18 drinks during the previous day, while an average female consumed 10 drinks. Binge drinking is higher among fraternity or sorority members, and among those who lead a party-centered lifestyle.

Students vacationing in groups are more likely to engage in pronounced substance abuse and in promiscuous sexual activity, which places them at a high risk of contracting sexually transmitted diseases. They might also engage in brawling, trespassing on waterfront properties, tearing down fences, and public urination.

Contributing factors

- A wish to get away from college and "winter blues"
- Opportunities afforded for easy socializing and new romantic involvements
- The anonymity afforded by spring breaks (at least in the minds of the students)
- The feeling of being a different person on holiday and, therefore, open to experiment with casual sex, drugs, and excessive drinking
- Commercial trip organizers encourage and facilitate visiting spring break destinations
- Commercial enterprises at resort destinations cater to spring break revelers

Examples of measures to curtail irresponsible behavior during spring breaks

Beachfront resorts in Destin, Florida, cooperated with local police by imposing a late night curfew on their private beaches during spring break. Several hotels floodlit their beaches to prevent trespassing, drinking, and other related behavior. In addition, police patrolled several miles of beach, concentrating where large crowds of teenagers might gather, stopping and making underage drinkers pour their beer onto the sand.

Police cameras were installed to monitor beaches and popular restaurants and bars in Sunset Beach, California. The police also increased uniformed and plainclothes patrols, set up DUI checkpoints, and enforced parking and traffic violations.

Residents of Pacific Beach, California, prevented a planned "pub crawl" by using a law prohibiting alcohol sales to intoxicated patrons. The organizers of the event pulled out after they received notice from the district's council member and the Department of Alcoholic Beverage Control, threatening to close down participating bars for 15 days should anyone be served alcohol who was already intoxicated.

Louisiana State University (LSU) held a "Smart & Safe Spring Break Festival" for students before spring break to provide them with abstinence information and information on health and safety issues. The university's police department deployed its motorcycle unit and K-9 bomb-sniffing dogs, performed intoxication demonstrations, and offered sign-ups for LSU's emergency text messaging and other services.

Inducements offered by bars to students at spring break

"all-you-can-drink" (generally a purchase of a meal is followed by unlimited beer and other alcoholic beverages)

"twofers" (offering two or more drinks for the price of one)

"coin nights" (involves flipping a coin, where the winner gets a free drink)

"ladies nights" (female customers are offered special discounts)

"bladder bursts" (promise of an enjoyable night—generally involving alcohol—where you don't want to miss anything by going to the bathroom)

"bar crawls" or **"bar hopping"** (going from one bar to another)

Operation Blitz' Em and Operation Spring Break in the Gold Coast, Australia, targeted speeding and drunk drivers during spring break. Random breath testing, unmarked cars, and speed cameras were deployed at hot spots and during high-risk times. Extra officers from the state traffic taskforce assisted local police.

What can you do?

Gather intelligence about the locations most likely to be visited by the students. Determine if these are mainly outdoors or indoors, and think of specific measures to address the issue based on the location type.

Identify bars with lenient underage drinking practices that might attract underage students during spring break.

Survey bars, restaurants, and motels that offer inducements to students at spring break and inform the owners and managers about possible dangers associated with these practices.

While students might bring their own drugs with them, there might be local supply sources that you need to identify and alert your police department about.

What can your agency do?

Control alcohol distribution by enforcing local ordinances against restaurant and bar owners, as well as alcohol vendors. Limit the number of liquor outlets during the spring break period. Working with vendors and bar owners to identify fake IDs can also help control underage drinking.

Establish police presence/visibility at and around locations identified as hot spots and monitor student behavior to ensure compliance with the law. The presence of uniformed police officers can help bring the situation under control by monitoring drinking, public nudity, drug use, and other related behaviors.

Partner with the local media to encourage and influence responsible student behavior while on spring break. Encourage the media to practice more socially responsible marketing efforts to promote healthier and safer spring break activities.

Local initiatives can involve offering financial rewards to individual "bounties" who report bars that serve intoxicated patrons, as well as underage students.

Provide free false-identification training for restaurant and bar employees to help reduce illegal sales to underage students.

Laws promoting responsible bar policies in certain states require servers, managers, and owners of restaurants and bars to attend a state-approved course every five years that includes information about alcohol's effect on the body, drunk-driving laws, effective server intervention techniques, and related topics. Similar programs can be implemented by your police department.

Warn potential offenders by posting signs specifying the ordinances (such as "nudity is prohibited in a public area") and that failure to follow these may lead to arrest.

Roads near the locations where spring breakers gather can be monitored by the police to discourage students from driving under the influence. Meanwhile, free shuttle services can be offered by the hotels to encourage safe travel. Consider closing certain streets.

Encourage universities to enforce disciplinary measures against students found to have engaged in binge drinking or drug use.

SINCE THE DEMONSTRATIONS AT THE 1999 MEETINGS OF THE WORLD TRADE ORGANIZATION IN SEATTLE, American police have increasingly been confronted with the problem of dealing with political protesters. There are four main kinds of political demonstrations:

1. **Marches**—proceeding from one location to another, such as the May 1, 2006, marches across the United States protesting the proposed immigration laws.

2. **Rallies**—gathering at a location to hear speakers or musicians, such as the November 3, 2007, student rally in Washington, D.C., to address issues on climate change and global warming.

3. **Picketing**—targeting a specific facility or building, such as the September 15, 2002, pickets at the Ukrainian Embassy in Washington, D.C., by the members of the Forum of Ukrainian Students of America, to honor Ukrainian journalists, and civil and political activists who had died after Ukrainian independence.

4. **Sit-ins/sit-downs**—nonviolent occupation of a building or public place and refusal to leave until demands have been met or an agreement reached. Sit-ins were widespread in the 1960s by African American college students across the United States campaigning to end racial segregation. A recent example is Occupy Wall Street in 2011.

Political demonstrations are generally peaceful, but violence and vandalism may occur, sometimes deliberately provoked by organizations such as the "Black Bloc", which exploit demonstrations to further their own political ends. Violent demonstrations are a particular problem for local police, as the inability to handle them properly may have serious implications for police-community relations.

The Black Bloc

- The Black Block is an international anarchist organization (also known as the Revolutionary Anti-Capitalist Bloc) started in Germany in 1987, which soon spread to the United States and Canada. Its unofficial center in America is Eugene, Oregon.

- It is best known for its violent demonstrations in Seattle in 1999 against the World Trade Organization. Other demonstrations include the 2001 demonstration at the Summit of the Americas in Quebec City, Canada; and the demonstrations in July 2001 in Genoa, Italy, at the General Assembly Summit. In recent years the Black Bloc has targeted such large American corporations as Banana Republic, Gap, Levi's, McDonald's, Old Navy, and Starbucks.

- Black Bloc protesters arrive at demonstrations dressed in three layers. The outermost layer is regular clothes worn at the beginning of the demonstration before the Black Bloc tactics are activated. The middle layer is all black clothing (and a black mask worn when the members are given the signal to engage in confrontation). The last layer involves regular clothes to escape from police.

- The Black Bloc often deploys in tight formations (in black) when confronting the police, or intimidating other groups.

Public-Order Policing

Aversion to disruption is used when police want to prevent demonstrations from interfering with the normal functioning of the city, for example, by denying the right to march on city streets and confining marches to sidewalks or to restricted areas and times of the day.

Controlling access involves the use of concrete or metal barriers to separate the protesters from the public and to control access through limited entry points.

Divide and conquer allows the police to have access to almost all parts of the demonstration by subdividing the crowds into smaller groups by the use of interlocking metal "french barriers." This makes it difficult for demonstrators to circulate freely, while allowing effective control of the crowds.

Shock and awe involves deploying a very large number of police officers to deter outbreaks of violence or other unlawful behavior. Police might employ less-than-lethal weapons to deal with protestors and commonly arrest leaders who promote violence or are themselves engaged in violence.

Zero tolerance involves the rigorous enforcement of legal statutes during demonstrations. Failure to comply with the provisions of a permit may be met by police in full riot gear shutting down sound systems and mass arrests of protesters at the expiration time of a permit to demonstrate.

Non-confrontational crowd management involves supporting the legitimate aims of demonstrators while avoiding confrontation that may alienate the crowd as a whole. Unruly or violent crowd members are carefully identified and removed by the police.

Dialogue policing is an extension of non-confrontational crowd management (Step 25). It aids communication between demonstrators and police commanders through specially-trained police officers in the crowd. This encourages self-policing among demonstrators, facilitates legitimate expression of freedom of speech and assembly, and prevents miscommunication between the police and demonstrators.

Source: Madensen and Knutsson 2010.

In most cases, your department will be called on to deal with smaller demonstrations that involve picketing or sit-ins. Sit-ins are common in administrative or congressional offices. For example, constituents may stage a sit-in in the office of their representative to protest his or her voting record. Sit-ins are especially common outside abortion and Planned Parenthood clinics.

Picketing is more common among employees who are dissatisfied with wages, long hours, working conditions, and related issues. Picketing will also sometimes be undertaken to block access to government buildings and corporations. Pickets are generally non-violent, but the police department's inability to handle the protests properly may lead to violent confrontations.

What can you do?

Stay informed about current political issues that may possibly become reasons for political demonstrations. Gather information on groups in your jurisdiction who are most likely to act on these issues. Study the backgrounds of these groups and determine their overall demonstration "style."

Political protesters use the Internet to voice their concerns, recruit new members, and to announce the locations and times where protests are to be held. Therefore, you can monitor the websites operated by these groups to gain understanding about their networks and activities. Some of these websites include:

- Infoshop www.infoshop.org

- Spunk Press www.spunk.org

- Anarchy Archives www.anarchyarchives.org

- Liberty for the People http://flag.blackened.net/liberty/liberty.html

- Noam Chomsky Archive www.zmag.org/chomsky/index.cfm

- Independent Media Center www.indymedia.org

Identify possible locations/targets, such as government buildings, corporate headquarters, financial institutions, and other symbolic buildings. Decide what strategies can be implemented and how these should differ from site to site and from group to group.

Gather information about strategies used by other police departments to handle similar situations. Determine if these strategies suit your police department's operational goals and whether any of the strategies would undermine community relations.

What can your agency do?

Police departments throughout the country have used a variety of approaches to control political demonstrators and other crowds (see *Public-Order Policing* on page 132). Which of these your department adopts in any particular situation may depend partly on its philosophy, but also on the groups they are dealing with.

Aggressive police intervention strategies may lead to violence in otherwise peaceful demonstrations, therefore, cooperative intervention is vital in controlling demonstrators. Keep in mind also, that advance changes to the setting can reduce damage. These include: blocking off streets and particular buildings; removing items such as building rubble that can be used as weapons; and temporary removal of street furniture such as trash cans that can be burned.

Lastly, your department can use electronic surveillance technologies to provide real-time information on demonstrations and quickly send in more police should the crowd turn violent.

READ MORE:

Tamara Madensen and Johannes Knutsson, eds. 2010. *Preventing Crowd Violence.* Vol. 26 of *Crime Prevention Studies.* Boulder, Colorado: Lynne Rienner Publishers, Inc.

PARTIES ARE ALMOST SYNONYMOUS WITH STUDENT LIFE, BUT IF UNREGULATED, THEY CAN RESULT IN BEHAVIORS requiring police intervention. These behaviors include underage drinking, binge drinking, drunk driving, sexual misconduct, fighting, sexual assaults, drugs, violence, noise, litter, and vandalism.

Studies of blood alcohol concentration levels have found that students at fraternity parties get significantly more intoxicated than those at other parties. In one large study of 140 colleges, 44 percent of the students surveyed reported binge drinking and 19 percent were frequent binge drinkers—those who binged three or more times in two weeks.

Common features of student parties

- The students present are mostly young adults—some may be under 21

- Alcohol is generally consumed in large amounts and drugs may also be used

- The parties begin late at night and may continue into the early morning

- Males are most often responsible for fighting or destructive behavior

- The parties may result in noise complaints from local residents

- Drunk driving is common

- Students may engage in unplanned or unprotected sexual activity

- Other young adults not associated with the college may also gather at the parties

- Students may get into trouble with campus or local police

The "life cycle" of student parties

Madensen and Eck report that the larger parties have a "life cycle" of five stages, around which police should organize their responses (see Table 18 on page 135).

Examples of what has been done to address the problem

Michigan State University used campaigns designed to challenge the attitudes and expectations of students regarding "celebration drinking." The campaigns made use of student and local newspapers and incorporated the distribution of flyers in campuses, student residences, and at Greek Life fairs.

The Robert Wood Johnson Foundation funded "A Matter of Degree" (AMOD) to reduce high-risk drinking among college students, which resulted in significant changes in drinking behaviors and decreases in related drunk driving, wild party complaints, and charges of maintaining a disorderly house.

Some police departments offer the "Adopt-the-Cop" program. This makes a police officer available at student gatherings to serve as a mentor and advisor to ensure compliance with city and college requirements for student parties.

In Minnesota, the Winona City Council passed an ordinance to control and track keg distribution. Anyone purchasing two or more half-barrels of beer in a residentially zoned area was required to obtain council approval, and liquor retailers were required to keep detailed records of barrels sold.

Rutgers University enforces good behavior at Greek parties through its Board of Control, which comprises fraternity and sorority students who check on parties in progress to ensure there is no vandalism, sexual misconduct, fighting, or other misbehavior. Local police train these students in how to handle violent situations, write up violations of school policy, and call the police in case of violence. Parties are limited to Friday and Saturday nights and require registration with the Fraternity Affairs Office and the local police department. The Board of Control checks out the party

Table 18. Five stages of large parties

STAGE	SUGGESTED RESPONSES
1. Initial Planning. Deciding to host a party, when and where; deciding whom to invite and how to invite them. Students are invited through flyers posted months in advance, word of mouth, or simple cues indicating that there will be a student party/gathering somewhere soon.	Create a multi-agency task force with other community stakeholders, most importantly with the college concerned. Require a permit for a party of more than a few friends. Assign police officers as advisors to hosts of gatherings.
2. Preassembly preparation. Obtaining alcohol and food by hosts or guests before the party.	Ask students to participate in "student patrols" by establishing "peer security" groups within the gathering. Monitor advertisements for gatherings.
3. Assembling process. Heading for the party. Students may drive, take a taxi or bus, or simply walk to the location.	Facilitate orderly gathering by providing transportation to the event. Establish a positive police presence, intended to reduce anonymity for police and students and enhance communication. Establish gathering perimeters in order to gain control of disturbances.
4. Assembled gathering. Having congregated, students talk, drink, and possibly engage in other behaviors associated with student parties.	Use alternative deployment methods, such as horses and bike patrols. Videotape the party to reduce anonymity. Develop a standard operating procedure in case of a disturbance.
5. Dispersal process. The party is over and students return to their dorms or apartments. Drunk driving may be a problem if students have reached the party in their own vehicles.	Provide transportation from the event to dorms or other centralized locations. Ask people to leave when the party is over.

Source: Madensen and Eck 2006.

three times a night, between the hours of 10:00 PM and 2:00 AM, where a checklist is completed about control measures such as checking IDs, using stamps or bracelets to identify guests, and keeping the noise down.

What can you do?

Study local college policies on controlling student parties and make contact with university administration should you need to find out more about these policies and how they are enforced.

Work closely with campus police or security to gather information on upcoming parties by monitoring student newspapers and student postings at college campuses.

Work with local student organizations to gather information about times of the day and days of the week parties are most likely to be held, how long they last, types of drinks consumed, how alcohol is obtained, whether drinking games are played, and any associated problematic behaviors.

Make contact with local college fraternities and sororities to find out more about the policies currently used to monitor and control Greek parties.

What can your agency do?

Discuss the alcohol policies effective on campus with local college administrators and suggest possible improvements should you find the college has problems effectively controlling student parties. Organize regular meetings/presentations on college campuses to discuss the dangers associated with irresponsible behavior at student parties.

Encourage colleges to give warnings and impose disciplinary actions against students who are engaged in disorderly conduct, violence, or other behaviors associated with student parties.

Form a partnership with student organizations and campus police/security to promote a safe party environment and responsible behavior at student parties. At the beginning of each academic year, discuss alcohol laws, off campus behavior, and other safety issues related to student parties with fraternity and sorority presidents.

Make clear to local bars, restaurants, and liquor outlets that sales to underage students will not be tolerated. Promote responsible beverage services, strengthen enforcement of drunk driving laws, and, where necessary, seek changes in local zoning ordinances to reduce the density of alcohol sales outlets.

Work with local rental property owners to require them to provide safe and secure apartments to students living off campus. Encourage them to call police in the event of problematic parties being held in their apartments.

READ MORE:

Tamara Madensen and John Eck. 2006. *Student Party Riots*. Problem-Oriented Guides for Police. Problem-Specific Guide Series, No. 39. Washington, D.C.: U.S. Department of Justice, Office of Community Oriented Policing Services.

About the Authors

John E. Eck

John Eck is a criminal justice professor at the University of Cincinnati, where he teaches police effectiveness, research methods, and crime prevention. His research has focused on the development of problem-oriented policing, police effectiveness, crime patterns, and crime prevention. Dr. Eck was a member of the National Academy of Science's Committee to Review Research on Police Policy and Practices. With Ronald Clarke, he authored *Crime Analysis for Problem-Solvers: In 60 Small Steps*. He is also the author of many publications on problem-oriented policing, crime mapping, and crime prevention, some written for the Center for Problem-Oriented Policing. Dr. Eck received his bachelor's and master's degrees from the University of Michigan, and his doctorate from the University of Maryland's Department of Criminology.

Ronald V. Clarke

Ronald Clarke is university professor at Rutgers University and associate director of the Center for Problem-Oriented Policing. He was previously head of the British government's criminological research department, where he had a significant role in the development of situational crime prevention and the British Crime Survey. Dr. Clarke is the founding editor of *Crime Prevention Studies*, and his publications include *Designing out Crime* (HMSO 1980), *The Reasoning Criminal* (Springer-Verlag 1986), *Situational Crime Prevention: Successful Case Studies* (Harrow and Heston 1997), *Superhighway Robbery: Preventing E-commerce Crime* (Willan Publishing 2003), *Outsmarting the Terrorists* (Praeger 2006), and with John Eck, *Become a Problem Solving Crime Analyst* (U.S. Department of Justice 2005). He was formerly chair of the selection committee for the annual Herman Goldstein Award for Excellence in Problem-Oriented Policing.

Gohar Petrossian

Gohar Petrossian is an assistant professor at John Jay College of Criminal Justice. She is the author of *Export of Stolen Vehicles across Land Borders* (Problem-Specific Guide No. 63, with Ronald V. Clarke), co-author of *Shoplifting (2nd Edition)* (Problem-Specific Guide No. 11, with Ronald V. Clarke), and scholarly articles published in *Journal of Experimental Criminology* and *Security Journal*. She holds a doctorate in criminal justice from the School of Criminal Justice, Rutgers University-Newark, and a master's in criminal law and procedure from John Jay College of Criminal Justice.

www.ingramcontent.com/pod-product-compliance
Lightning Source LLC
Chambersburg PA
CBHW080256290526
45790CB00005B/1830